Lewis O. Thompson, Abbott E. Kittredge

The Prayer-Meeting and its Improvement

Lewis O. Thompson, Abbott E. Kittredge

The Prayer-Meeting and its Improvement

ISBN/EAN: 9783337284503

Printed in Europe, USA, Canada, Australia, Japan

Cover: Foto ©Lupo / pixelio.de

More available books at **www.hansebooks.com**

THE
PRAYER-MEETING

AND

ITS IMPROVEMENT.

BY

REV. LEWIS O. THOMPSON,

PASTOR SECOND PRESBYTERIAN CHURCH, PEORIA, ILL.

WITH AN INTRODUCTION BY

REV. A. E. KITTREDGE.

"Let all things be done unto edifying."

CHICAGO:
W. G. HOLMES,
77 MADISON STREET.

TO THE CONGREGATION

OF THE

Second Presbyterian Church,

PEORIA, ILL.,

THIS VOLUME

IS AFFECTIONATELY INSCRIBED BY

THEIR PASTOR.

PREFACE.

This book is designed as a go-between, between pastor and people, to call their combined attention to some hints and principles that would enlarge the efficiency of the prayer-meeting, and to assure those to whom public speaking is a burden, that their experience is common to the majority of mankind, and should give them no uneasiness, beyond spurring them on until they acquire the habit of extempore speech.

If the prayer-meeting is to be more than a mere side-show to the church, if it is to rise into one of the great departments of successful Christian work, there must be as much thought, prayer and effort given to it, as to either of the Sabbath services or the Sabbath school. What is needed in many cases is such a method for its conduct, and such a hearty co-operation of all in that method, as shall make the prayer-meeting, both in interest and attendance, an undoubted success.

May the Lord bless for good whatever of truth these chapters contain, and make them instrumental in stirring up the zeal of the churches to untiring labor and faithful prayer in the advancement of His cause.

Go little book—if God shall be pleased to commission thee—from church to church as an evangelist in the cause of the Prayer-Meeting and its Improvement.

LEWIS O. THOMPSON.

PEORIA, ILL.

CONTENTS.

Chapter		Page
I.	The Prayer-Meeting as a Subject of Study,	11
II.	The People's Meeting,	16
III.	The Need of Preparation,	22
IV.	The Daily Cultivation of Piety,	33
V.	The Topics,	42
VI.	The Topics Illustrated,	49
VIII.	One Method for the Selection of Topics,	67
IX.	Bible Readings for the Prayer-Meeting,	75
X.	Illustrations of Bible Readings,	82
XI.	A Plan for Each Meeting,	93
XII.	Variety in Successive Meetings,	104
XIII.	The Importance of the Prayer-Meeting,	110
XIV.	How to Make Prayer-Meetings Interesting,	116
XV.	Uniform Topics,	122
XVI.	Steps Towards Uniformity,	131
XVII.	Helps to Speaking in Public,	145
XVIII.	How to Secure Attendance,	159
XIX.	How Prayer-Meetings are Kept at a White Heat,	168
XX.	Treatment of the Monthly Concert,	172
XXI.	Laying Out Work,	176
XXII.	Hints New and Old,	186
XXIII.	Daily Prayer-Meeting Topics,	196

INTRODUCTION.

It is impossible to over-estimate the value of the prayer-meeting, as it stands related to the life and usefulness of the Church of Christ. In fact, no other service can be compared with this in importance—not even the Sabbath preaching, nor the instruction in the Sunday-school—for without a live prayer-meeting the church will be spiritually cold, the Sabbath services will be formal, and the children will be fed with husks instead of provisions from the Master's table.

The weekly prayer-meeting is the pulse of the church,—one of the most encouraging signs of the times, in the religious world, is the increased interest manifested by pastors and churches in this topic, and the new life and power which now are found in many of these hallowed circles of united prayer and praise. Some of us can remember the prayer-meetings of our childhood, when the number present ranged from ten to twenty or thirty, and most of these were the female members—when the leader occupied most of the hour in cold, doctrinal remarks, and then remarked: "Brethren, the meeting is open," after which came the solemn pauses, only broken by this and that good deacon taking pity on the meeting, and making a few forced and uninteresting remarks. Oh! how cold those meetings were! cold enough to freeze up any longings to be a Christian, in the breast of a sinner who might have chanced to happen in. How we children used to dread being compelled to attend, preferring even to go to bed earlier than usual, rather than to sit for an hour in that spiritual refrigerator. Such prayer-meetings are, we trust, seldom found now, for with the increased interest in the Sabbath-school, the weekly meeting has been steadily growing in importance, in the estimation of Christians of all denominations.

Now, upon whom shall we lay the blame for a lifeless prayer-meeting? The safest course is to distribute it all round, for usually pastor and church members are all at fault—the pastor for a lack of preparation, the people for a lack of co-operation. By lack of preparation we do not mean as regards careful thought upon the chapter to be read, for we hold most firmly that one of the chilling influences in such a meeting is the lengthy and elaborate "opening" by the pastor, leaving nothing for the brethren to say, and dampening all enthusiasm to speak. The pastor should simply open the meeting, and read the chapter, saying nothing, unless it be a single thought to give direction to the thoughts of others. His remarks will come in better at the close, when he can occupy five minutes in gathering up the suggestions which have been uttered, and, perhaps, add one or more practical lessons not mentioned by others.

Then the pastor's opening remarks are apt to be more theological than experimental, and they serve to seal the lips of those whose theological education may be deficient, but whose experience of the preciousness of Christ may be very rich.

Then, again, the pastor has an opportunity twice on the Sabbath to instruct the church on theological truths, but the prayer-meeting belongs peculiarly to the people,—it is *their* hour, not *his*, and therefore, it is stealing from them their property, when one-half of the time is occupied by the pastor, who should simply lead and control the exercises. But the pastor may prepare for this meeting by a wise selection of two or three persons, to whom he will state the chapter to be read, so that they will be *ready* to speak as soon as he takes his seat, thus avoiding pauses which kill a prayer-meeting, and making sure the interest of the remarks made. It may happen that these selected speakers will have no chance to speak—so much the better—but they will be ready to fill any possible gap, and their earnest words will kindle an inspiration in other hearts and will open other lips. In this selection, the same persons should not be often called on; and there should be a difference of age between them, so that the young, as well as the older, will feel that the pastor looks to them for the support of the meeting. The wisdom of such a course will be apparent when we remember that our business men come to the evening meeting from the cares and anxieties of the counting-room, and it can hardly be expected that they will be ready to speak at once on spiritual matters, unless they have been able to prepare their minds, by a knowledge of the passage to be read.

Then, in regard to the exercises of the hour, we often err in running our prayer-meetings in a stereotyped form so that they become dry and uninteresting—the same thing week after week. There should be plenty of singing,—not an entire hymn, but a verse thrown in between the prayers and remarks. Our people love to sing, and while but few may be able to speak, all can praise God in song. Dispense with the instrument, if possible, but if it is used, do not let precious moments be occupied by playing the melody all through, or by interludes, which are always a serious infliction on the people. Insist that the remarks be very brief, not more than three minutes, and if the brother is burdened to say more, let him keep it carefully for another time. Three minutes are long enough for the utterance of one thought, and this is all that any one person should give in a meeting of only one hour's duration. Have more praying than talking. Many a so-called prayer-meeting is no *prayer*-meeting at all, but is all talk, talk, talk—and it is no wonder they are dull and powerless. The purpose of these gatherings of the church is to gain spiritual strength, and prayer is the grand channel through which this strength can be received; and, therefore, make the hour *full of prayer—short* prayers, earnest, simple prayers but a great many of them. But we are exceeding the limits of an introductory article, and close with urging upon all who love the Church of Christ, and desire its spiritual health and purity and power, to love the prayer-meeting, to seek its increasing interest, so that it shall be the grand spiritual armory of believers, and the very gate of heaven to many, many souls.

May this little book have a blessed mission among the churches!

A. E. KITTREDGE.

THE PRAYER-MEETING
AND ITS IMPROVEMENT.

CHAPTER I.

THE PRAYER-MEETING AS A SUBJECT OF STUDY.

How to improve the prayer-meeting may not seem so serious a question to our large and prosperous city churches. Evidently it is easier for them to conduct the meetings to general satisfaction and edification than for some of the smaller country churches. They have a membership running up to many hundreds, and out of that number many who are fluent speakers, both by culture and profession; whilst in the country the conditions are less favorable, both because the membership is often below a hundred, and there are not in that number more than half a dozen who are in the habit of taking a part in the exercises of the meeting. Now, under such circumstances, the charge and improvement of the prayer-meeting becomes a serious question.

It is almost an axiom that the successful prayer-meeting will make the successful church; and it is equally true that if the prayer-meeting is not a success, it can be made so. There are principles which apply to its conduct, just as well as to successful business or school-keeping. As a matter of course, I would look for no success which is not connected with the Bible and with Bible methods, and which does not depend upon the Holy Spirit for its inspiration.

It may be true, also, that the precise method which would insure success to one church, might not, without some modification, do the same for another. There are differences in culture between different congregations. But whatever the method pursued, it should be such, that while it is continuously improving the prayer-meeting, it shall at the same time improve the intellectual and spiritual condition of the church.

The prayer-meeting is all too generally a place to which many laymen go "with fear and trembling." With many it is a comfortless thing; for they are fearing all the time that their pastor will see them and call upon them: "Well, Brother Blank, how is it with you? I hope you will testify. Haven't you got a word to say? Or, will you not lead us in prayer?" I think I know why there are more women to attend prayer-meeting than men. They do not have to speak, and for them, doubtless, there is peace and comfort in the exercises. I have known men who have sat through a prayer-meeting in a sort of cold chill, with nerves unstrung, wishing the minister would omit them; looking solemn and anxious, until the benediction descended upon them with a joy almost indescribable. There are men so constituted that a call upon them to speak or pray seems to send every idea they ever had to the four quarters of the compass; and when, in obedience to the call, they do arise, though it be the coldest kind of weather, the sweat starts and runs in rivulets. "Why, sir," said one of the best men in the world, "if I was to undertake to repeat the Lord's Prayer when called upon in meeting, I don't think I could do it; and yet I know it as well as my own name." A man of a very nervous and sensitive temperament would almost as soon have a tooth pulled as to attend prayer-meeting and sit through the terrible ordeal. In such cases, attendance upon a prayer-meeting becomes more a duty than a pleasure.

Nor is it anything against a man that may be bashful, timid, or unused to public speaking, if his first trials should prove failures. There have been able men and profound thinkers who have been unable to think and speak fluently before an audience. Indeed, it is a matter of history that some of the most brilliant orators in their "maiden speeches" have completely failed.

And then, besides this, there is another thing to be borne in mind, and that is this: the public does not have the same knowledge of our mental states that we ourselves possess. Some men judge of the effect of their remarks or prayers by their own feelings, and because these are depressed, they think they cannot speak to edification, and so had better keep still. Their thoughts, while they are on their feet, seem to be flying about in utter confusion, like flakes in a snow-storm, and they feel that others must be as painfully conscious of their agitation as they themselves are.

How, then, can we assist such men as these to take part with greater pleasure to themselves and profit to others? How can we assure the timid that practice will soon confirm their nerves, and give them a more orderly command of their thoughts while upon their feet, and in the presence of the terrifying audience? How can we conduct the meetings so as to make them comfortable for all, and cause them to abound in spiritual refreshment and Christian fellowship? How can we discover just the method for our particular charges, that will wake up the mind of all, stimulate Bible reading and research, as well as stir up their zeal to renewed activity in all departments of Christian work? How can we make available for the good of the church just such talent as our members now possess? How can we secure the attendance of all the membership upon the prayer-meeting? In a word, how can we make our prayer-meeting "The Model Prayer-Meeting?"

The cause of Christ and the welfare of the church at large emphasize these and related questions, and demand from every minister that he make their solution the subject of special study, and the improvement of the prayer-meeting a matter of prayerful and untiring endeavor. The following pages are offered as a series of hints in this direction.

CHAPTER II.

THE PEOPLE'S MEETING.

THE prayer-meeting on some evening of the week is the people's meeting. The Sabbath is the day for the ministration of the pastor. They each have their day. If it is not wise for the people to conduct the services of the Sabbath, neither is it wise for the pastor to monopolize the exercises of the week-day meeting. If it is true that the active piety of a church rises no higher than it manifests itself in the prayer-meeting, so that here, as on a barometer, all changes in spiritual life are faithfully recorded, then certainly too much attention cannot be given by both pastor and people to the conduct of the prayer-meeting.

The people need just such a meeting as the week-day meeting is, and ought to be, and what it can be made to be, if it is not already. There is so little place given in our churches on Sunday for the participation of the people in its services; and hence so many have come to regard the day as an entertain-

THE PRAYER-MEETING. 17

ment in eloquence and music. If these are wanting, if they cannot hear a fine sermon from one end of the church, and be soothed by sweet music from the other, they will not go to church—no, not they. But offer them a lecture and a concert agreeably combined, they may consent to go. Where this idea prevails, the people have forgotten that on Sunday they are to publicly appear before God, to render unto Him worship, prayer, praise and thanksgiving, with the confession of their sins and the earnest supplication for new supplies of grace; and all this they can do, though the sermon be never so feeble and the singing never so poor. But the people need a meeting in which to tell their experience, comfort one another, pray for one another, and, where the case requires it, bear one another's burdens. Life in the market and the domestic circle, in the shop and the store, in the kitchen and the school-room, in the street and the field, at home and abroad, has its trials and burdens, its anxieties and sorrows, its temptations and defeats, as well as its joys and triumphs. Griefs are lessened and joys are multiplied when others share them with us.

> "Thoughts shut up want air,
> And spoil, like bales unopened to the sun."

How precious, then, is the privilege that admits us to the circle of congenial friends and steadfast companions on the road from earth to heaven. Here they meet to "rejoice with them that do rejoice, and weep with them that weep;" and so, by mutual vows and endeavors and sympathies, fainting hearts are made resolute, and the tread of uncertain feet firm and victorious.

> "As bees mix'd nectar draw from fragrant flow'rs,
> So men from friendship, wisdom and delight."

How eagerly the fainting Israelite gathered the freshly-fallen manna! With what alacrity did not the thirsty tribes bound forward as the majestic palm-trees arose before them in the distance—seventy palm-trees, as they clustered around the twelve springs of Elim, and fed their roots around these living fountains—how joyously, we may imagine, did not the air resound with shouts of "Water! water! there is water at the roots of the palm-trees!" When the traveler is about to sink beneath the heat and the thirst of his journey through the arid wastes, he sees just before him the green oasis, and starts forward with renewed hope to reach its shade and refreshment. When the summer's heat is oppressive, and to breathe is burdensome, how gladly mankind seeks the cooling beach of lake or

THE PRAYER-MEETING.

sea, or the green swards, the cooling glens, and the shady trees, rich in leaf and fruit, as these may be found amid the lawn, the field and the forest.

Ought not the prayer-meeting on the midday of the week to be all this to the Christian, who, having set his face Zionward, is making the journey to the celestial city; yes, more than all these to him, whose feet cannot rest till they walk in safety thy golden streets, O Jerusalem! Ought not the prayer-meeting to be the tree with fruit and foliage—the common on which feet are cooled as they walk and sink into the grassy carpet—the oasis with its refreshment—Elim with its seventy palm-trees and twelve fountains of water that never run dry—the company of friends where words may be opened to the sun, where criticism shall be disarmed, and what we desire to say shall be better understood than what we do say, if for any reason our words are inadequate?

And just an instance to show what freedom and friendliness characterize the prayer circle may not be out of place here. Not long ago I attended a prayer meeting in Chicago. Both pastor and people were strangers to me. As the meeting was nearing its close, a convert got up to speak. He was full of love and zeal, as all converts are, but he was evidently unused to public speaking. His hands were kept flying constantly and all about his head as if fighting an imaginary wasp's nest, whilst his body kept bobbing up and down all the time in a ludicrous manner. Most certainly he satisfied that rule of eloquence which makes it consist in a threefold action; and besides all this, his English was quite broken, and so rapidly spoken that it was difficult to catch word and sense. Did they laugh? Not exactly; a smile or two may have been suppressed, but that was all. Anywhere else he would have been greeted with uproarious laughter. Here however, we all felt like going up to the brother to thank him for his remarks and bid him God-speed in his efforts. It is more fit that criticism should sleep in the prayer circle than the members. Whoever feels called upon to pray or speak, may do so in the feeling that all will be kindly received, and that nothing but generous sympathy awaits him.

The prayer-meeting, then, is the people's meeting, and they support its exercises. Here they witness for Christ; here they renew their consecration; here is the place where much good may be done and much good received by words of encouragement and sympathy; and as such the people should relish its opportunities and not neglect its privileges. Had not Thomas been absent from just one meeting of the disciples, he would have received, eight days earlier than he did, the proof he required to save him from skepticism; and had he absented himself continuously, he might have died in unbelief.

People are to put themselves in the way of receiving the blessings of God; for the church in its ordinances is the channel of grace, and our spiritual wants will be best ministered unto when we are most constant in our attendance upon all the meetings. And it may prove in our case as in that of Thomas, that the meetings we miss are the very ones which contain the thoughts, the prayers, the songs, and the experiences for lack of which our souls are famishing, and we are subjected to those temptations which weaken rather than confirm our faith.

"I've found a glad hosanna
  For every woe and wail;
A handful of sweet manna
  When grapes of Eshcol fail;
I've found a Rock of Ages
  When desert wells are dry;
And after weary stages,
  I've found an Elim nigh.

My Saviour, Thee possessing,
  I have found the joy, the balm,
The healing and the blessing,
  The sunshine and the psalm;
The promise for the fearful,
  The Elim for the faint;
The rainbow for the tearful,
  The glory for the saint!"

CHAPTER III.

Preparation.

The pastor does not presume to enter the pulpit Sabbath after Sabbath without proper preparation. He has a very low view of his duty, the dignity of the pulpit, as well as of the privilege and pleasure of preaching, who thinks anything is good enough for the pulpit, and is willing to rush before his people, as the horse to battle, with stray scraps of thought. When Dr. Beecher once preached to the students of Andover, and was asked how long it took him to prepare that sermon, he replied in his peculiar way, "Twenty years." The full sermon comes from the full preparation and years of study lying back of it.

The pastor cannot rely upon inspiration to take the place of study, nor look for a miracle to supply him text and thought at the time he is to preach. It is true that the disciples were to take no thought as to what they should say when brought before magistrates, for in the same hour they should be told what to say. Emergencies and exceptional cases will often arise when the preacher will have to rely upon God for his sermon entirely; and then the sermon comes to him not as a substitute for his fidelity but in connection with it, and because more will be accomplished by it than by that which could have been premeditated. At one of the places in which Rev. C. C. Finney was holding revival services, an infidel club was formed, it is said, for the purpose of opposing Christian work. The leader was a physician, who, on one occasion, slipped into the church and seated himself in the choir. Mr. Finney, coming in, and, as usual, glancing about his audience, saw this man, and at once changed his text, and preached that morning a powerful sermon on the plan of salvation, taking as his text: "For God so loved the world that He gave His only-begotten Son that whosoever believeth on Him should not perish, but have everlasting life." In the afternoon the Doctor came again, and the sermon, on the text, "How shall we escape if we neglect so great salvation?" seemed to be the logical sequence of the morning's sermon. In the evening the Doctor was again present, and the sermon was a conclusion of the whole matter, from the text, "But they made light of it." A lady spoke to the Doctor at the close of the service:

"Doctor, you've heard the truth; now, are you going away to-night to make light of it?" "No, ma'am, I am not," was his reply. That night he tried to sleep, but at midnight rose and paced the room, until he cried to his wife: "Wife, I can't live so, and I won't live so." The next day he stood up in the meeting, his powerful frame quivering with emotion, and said: "Look at me! What's this? It's God, and I'm a sinner!" Riding that day, he met one of his infidel friends on the road and stopped him. "Whedon," said he, "do you think there are any good men?" "Yes, of course I do." "Whedon, do you think all men are good?" "Yes, I do." "Whedon, don't you think there are some wicked men?" "No, I don't." "Whedon, you *lie*, and you *know* you lie;" and then the Doctor rode rapidly on."

Now, as Mr. Finney was in the habit of going from place to place to labor as an evangelist, he no doubt had a number of sermons prepared for this especial work, and the inference is a fair one that these sermons had the logical sequence which study and perhaps previous use had given them, and having many arrows in his quiver, he would naturally select those that would be best adapted to reach certain persons in his audience.

The example of the disciples is exceptional, of course; for they had a particular promise to rely upon. In their missionary labors they would encounter dangers and difficulties too great for human prudence and premeditation to remove, and therefore the promise of the Holy Spirit to assist them gave peace and quiet to their minds, and sent them forward in their labors with hope and courage. God will supply all need in the hour of emergency; "for without Me ye can do nothing"—but God does not promise to do for us what He designs we shall do for ourselves. As relates to diligence, study and preparation, their need is well expressed in that Cromwellian motto, "Trust in God, but keep your powder dry."

But as the prayer-meeting, in the main, is the people's meeting, it is hardly necessary to ask if they need preparation for its exercises? And to give this pointed application, we may ask ourselves, "For what purpose do we attend the prayer-meeting?" When we clearly understand its object, we shall better see to what extent preparation is necessary.

This meeting is needed in order that the religious life of the church may find public expression by the people themselves. Soldiers come together that they may drill and perfect themselves in the manual of arms. Soldiers who cannot execute the commands of the officer with alacrity and uniformity would make a sorry army, and but little headway against an enemy well-officered and in a state of splendid discipline. The people should come together, that like comrades they may stand shoulder to shoulder, and by the expression of their trials and victories, their confessions and their aspirations, and their words of prayer and praise, they may go through the exercises of the spiritual manual, and learn how good a thing fellowship is, and what a blessed privilege the communion of saints forms for us here below; and in thus sharing our experiences of joy and sorrow, of faith, hope and love, they may learn the better to keep step together in the Christian life, and make our conflict with the world, the flesh and the devil more victorious.

The people need this meeting as an aid to growth in grace. The experience of every Christian will show that his seasons of most rapid progress in the Christian walk and in the attainment of the Christian graces coincide with the seasons when he was faithful in the use of means, regular in attendance upon the ordinances of God's house and the prayer-meeting, and when his voice was lifted up to praise God in company with his brethren. Times of backsliding and lukewarm indifference will be found to have been those in which he neglected the means of grace, and when what he considered of more importance kept him from the prayer-meeting. Guerilla warfare does not equal that service which is regular and systematic.

The people need the prayer-meeting for the cultivation of the devotional spirit. Songs of praise acquire a power when tuned by many voices, and especially so if they are sung with the spirit and the understanding. Words of prayer, however simple, if heartfelt, possess a reflex influence and a new power from the assenting presence of the brethren. When "amen," either audibly or silently, is added to the prayer, it becomes the prayer of all, and receives force from that very circumstance. God does not judge the prayer by the graces of rhetoric and the rules of grammar, but by its faith and sincerity. "Likewise the Spirit also helpeth our infirmities: for we know not what we should pray for as we ought; but the Spirit itself maketh intercession for us with groanings which cannot be uttered." Words without heart in them, however eloquent otherwise, never find their way to heaven, but rise about as high as the head. We are blessed in the attendance of those meetings—our faith is confirmed, our love is warmed, and our hope is encouraged—the whole life is progressively sanctified—which are marked by the absence of formal praise and stilted prayers. From such meetings, where our hearts have melted under divine love, where our souls have been refreshed with heavenly manna and water flowing from the living Rock, one does not think of rushing to places of frivolity and worldly amusement.

When Moses was coming down from the mount where he had communed with God during forty days, and the wicked and thoughtless frivolity and idolatry of his people met his gaze, his soul was filled with righteous indignation, and the two tables of stone were dashed in pieces at his feet. The contrast was too great and too sudden—communion with God in its power and sweetness on the one hand, and gross superstition and naked idolatry on the other.

The people need the prayer-meeting that they may have an opportunity, in the spirit of Heb. 10 : 24, 25, to study each other with special reference to temperment and peculiarities, and that so they may be able more readily to provoke each the other unto love and to good works. Such provocation as shall make the fruit of the Spirit grow and ripen is not only permissible, but even commendable. The Christian is to regard his brethren as text-books for study, with the view of constantly improving them in the nurture of every needed grace and virtue.

And if the pastor should ask, how can I do more than I am already doing, it might be suggested that he give a whole day to planning and preparing for each meeting. Monday is generally considered a "blue" day with ministers. It would seem that this day might be turned to good account in many ways. Suppose he spend this day in visiting his people, and following up a little the impressions produced by his Sabbath ministrations. He would receive many a stimulating word and suggestion that would help him in his work for the next Sabbath; and while the iron is thus hot, he might make some good hits for the coming prayer-meeting, and get a limited number to promise and come especially prepared with reference to a given topic. As he visits from house to house there will arise special cases of spiritual need and sympathy; formulate such cases as these and make each one the topic for special prayer. Ask some one to come and pray for one who may be sick; another one to pray for one peculiarly tempted; another to pray for himself that he may receive grace and strength to labor for the salvation of some friend with whom he may have especial influence. In this way not only particular cases of need in a congregation will be prayed for, and doubtless with the most beneficial results; but also new topics for special prayer will constantly arise to keep pace with the steady and healthy growth in grace of the whole church, and enlarge the sphere of its influence and usefulness.

Finally, let each one that the pastor asks to take a part come early to the meeting, and as *soon as he gets a chance, after the introductory services, arise and pray, or offer remarks.* In this way there will be a rapid movement in the meeting like the tramp of an army on the march, and with something of the rapid scenes which characterizes the Gospel of St. Mark who takes us from "the beginning of the Gospel of Jesus Christ" on until "the Lord was received up into heaven," in sixteen chapters. Upon such a church as this,—a church realizing that it is "not by might, nor by power, but by my Spirit," and earnestly seeking to know the mind of the Spirit—God will pour, according to His promise, a burden of prayer, and guide it into such a path of success as shall keep it in constant revival.

Now it may be that prayer-meetings are not more largely attended and more generally successful because both pastor and people allow them to take care of themselves, with the feeling that the odds and ends of thought—the apple-parings and peach stones—gathered from second-hand experience will be good enough for the week-day meeting. Life, experience, and the best thoughts from the history which each one is writing of himself is what we want for the prayer-meeting, and such songs as shall express our faith, love and aspiration. If this field is to bear a large harvest, it must be faithfully worked. He who spends the most time in the cultivation of his farm, who uses the best seed with a liberal sowing is the one that secures the best harvest and the largest income. Weeds are about the only things that need no cultivation.

Nor should this chapter be closed without presenting the need of continuous preparation on the part of all. The people should be diligent and life-long students of the Bible that they may be accumulating a treasury from which, like the prudent housekeeper, to "bring forth things both new and old." They ought to be constant in the use of secret prayer, and all the stated means of grace which God has provided for the support and growth of spiritual life. "When thou wast under the fig tree I saw thee." They ought likewise to endeavor every day to lead a consistent and victorious Christian life. This will give depth and flavor to their experience, and make prayer and praise the joyful expression of their daily life.

And when you go to the prayer-meeting go to it from your knees with the earnest petition that God will hear and answer. "Be filled with the Spirit."

CHAPTER IV.

The Daily Cultivation of Piety.

There are some who seem to hate religion. They will not enter the Kingdom themselves, nor permit others to enter it, if they can prevent it by their words and opposition. There are some who seem indifferent about religion. It does not matter to them, one way or another, whether Christianity is true or false. Life in the present is so busy and so full of cares that if they can only make a living now, they will let the life in the hereafter take care of itself. They will run their chances. There are some who have a great respect for religion. They give liberally to the support of the Gospel. If their children are converted and unite with the church, they are glad. They know their children will grow up to be better men and women if they become religious. Such are like "Noah's carpenters,"—they help to build the ark, but neglect to enter it themselves. Some are willing that their wives shall be religious, but their own case is such they cannot attend to religion just now. They are in pursuit of wealth, or pleasure, or ambition. If they should become religious, it would require a change in their business; or if not that, at least a change in the manner of conducting it. For the present, you must have them excused. When they have a convenient season they will send for you.

There are others who profess religion, but do not prosecute it with any zeal. Their religion is for Sunday. They attend church regularly, but when the doors of the church are closed, their hearts are closed also, and during the week they give themselves up to the worldly spirit. There are others who add company religion to this Sunday religion. Such are not anxious to entertain ministers or earnest Christians at their homes during the holding of religious meetings and conventions; because this requires of them that they should have family worship morning and evening. But they are hospitable, and so, for the time being, they dust their Bibles, oil their knees, and kindle a fire upon the family altar. And there are others, also, whose religion is a proxy religion. They are reverential; they daily bend the knees at family worship, and are constant in attendance upon all the ordinances of God's house; but they never pray themselves. Others do the praying for them in the family, in the prayer-meeting, and in the church. They may silently or audibly say "Amen," but as for themselves, they neither pray in public, in private, nor in secret. They are prayerless Christians.

Why is it that religion is not relished more than appears to be the case? Why, in so many cases, is it that Christian life is so feeble? Is it because religion has come to be merely professional? Let a physician be called, and though he be ever so kind and gentle, yet he is apt from long practice to look at the patient and his disease from a professional standpoint, rather than enter fully into sympathy with him as a man and a brother.

During the late civil war it became my opportunity, as a member of the Sanitary Commission, to attend upon some wounded soldiers, as they were being taken by steamboat from White House Landing, Va., to Washington. There were some fifteen of us to take care of 405 men. Two surgeons of the regular army accompanied us. I became greatly interested in the case of a poor fellow whose wound was in a bad condition, and needed skillful and instant attention. I endeavored to get one of the doctors to do something for him. He came, and after making some experiments to ascertain the extent of the injury, he stated that he could not do anything for him, as he was in need of a particular instrument. You must wait till you get to Washington. Now there was something in the manner so heartless and indifferent that I was astonished. For myself, I could get no sleep during those sixty hours that we were on that boat. We who had volunteered to take care of those men, felt their sufferings to be a terrible strain upon our nervous system. We were unused to such sights and sufferings, and the amount of sympathy called for was almost more than we could endure.

Now, it may be that something like this takes place in our religious experience. After a while we lose its early fervor. Our religion ceases to be new, fresh, emotional and inspirational; it becomes professional. I remember during a revival at college when I first began to feel the new life in its preciousness—in its fullness of promise, hope and inheritance—how near the Saviour seemed to be. As I was going to my room after one of the evening meetings, everything appeared to be new. "Old things are passed away; behold all things are become new." It was a lovely evening. I looked up into the sky, and the stars were twinkling with a friendly lustre I had never noticed before. The thought that all these things are mine, because I am His, took possession of my soul. "All are yours; and ye are Christ's, and Christ is

God's." If the child of nature in a moment of enthusiasm can say, as he looks up at the sun, its rays glittering from the leaves of the over-arching trees in the grove, " This is my air, my sunshine, my earth;" how much more truly may not the child of God, as he beholds the works of his Father's hand, exclaim, "My air, my stars, my earth!"

Now, how can we return to a state like this of tender susceptibility, if we have lost it? I can never forget how deeply I was impressed, during my school days, by the example of a devout Christian, whose heart seemed so full of love, that he never could mention the name of the Saviour without a tear starting from his eyes and his lips quivering with emotion. How can we live so as to enjoy religion every hour of the day? Can the answer be otherwise than by the daily and careful cultivation of piety? Set apart half an hour every day for secret prayer and the devotional study of God's Word. I should like to ask for an entire hour; but I ask for half an hour in the hope that when that much has been given, the season will be so fully relished and found so precious that a full hour will be gladly taken. Such daily habit will prevent the religious life from becoming "stale, flat, unprofitable" and professional merely.

Seek to be alone at such a time; "When thou

prayest, enter into thy closet, and when thou hast shut thy door, pray to thy Father, which is in secret; and thy Father which seeth in secret shall reward thee openly." And let it be the first half-hour in the day; for "the morning hour has gold in its mouth." Let the first half hour of the day "before food, before family, before daily avocation, be made sacred to the Lord."

God has given us three most valuable gifts—His Word, His Son and His Spirit. We need to study the Word, because the Holy Spirit uses that as an instrument to communicate God's Will, to convince and convert, and to edify and sanctify our "whole spirit, soul and body." The Holy Spirit glorifies Christ in the Word. We need to study it therefore and to pray over it. God is the object of our worship, Christ is the basis of our worship, the Holy Spirit is the agency of our worship—our Guide, Teacher and Comforter—and the Word is the Instrument. And so the Word of God will furnish holy themes for the "secret hour." Like fuel cast upon fire, these will feed the flame of devotion, and cause it to glow with a steady light.

And now the practice of spending such a season—the first moments of the day—in secret prayer and communion with God, has been a habit with many eminent men and devoted Christians.

"It is said of one of our most eminent statesmen, at a time when most responsible duties to the country rested on him, that his morning hour was always spent in imploring the help of the Great Ruler of the Nations. A distinguished judge acknowledged his success in his profession as owing to the hour he daily spent with God. General Havelock, though burdened with the care of the army during the terrible mutiny in India, managed to keep sacred for prayer a long time in the morning of each day. Other names might be added, as those of Bacon, and the great astronomer Kepler, and the historian De Thou, of whom it is related, every morning, he implored God in private to purify his heart, to banish from it hatred and flattery, to enlighten his mind, and to make known to him the truth which so many passions and conflicting interests had almost buried. This was also the custom of one, guided by the Divine Spirit, for David's resolution was: 'My voice shalt thou hear in the morning, O Lord; in the morning will I direct my prayer unto thee, and will look up.' The testimony of that most godly man, Philip Henry, speaking of one of his studying days, was: 'I forgot, when I began, explicitly and expressly to crave help from God, and the chariot-wheels drove accordingly. Lord forgive my omission, and keep me in the way of duty!'

What higher example and encouragement could we have for this practice?"—*Dr. Murphy.*

And there are those who do not find the morning season sufficient for the daily wants of the spiritual life, after such a practice has once become fixed. In the Methodist Church Block in Chicago, before the great fire, "there was a certain dark closet under a stairway, used for the storage of wood and coal," which, as every other nook and corner of the building was occupied, Moody and his earnest co-laborers used as a closet for secret prayer. There, alone or in company, these devout Christians used to shut themselves up, and while the great business world rolled around them, above and below, like the sea around Jonah, they held sweet communinon with their Lord. Rev. Chas. G. Finney states in his Autobiography, that he discovered while a guest in the house of Anson G. Phelps, that this distinguished merchant of New York was in the habit of arising, after having taken a nap, to secretly hold communion with his God. "Seven times a day do I praise thee," says the sweet singer of Israel. Three times a day did Daniel kneel in his chamber with his "windows open toward Jerusalem." Sir Thomas Browne wrote in his journal as an admonition to himself, " to be sure to let no day pass without calling upon God in a solemn-formed prayer seven times within the compass thereof: that is, in the morning and at night and five times between."

Be sure to begin the day aright, and from such daily cultivation of piety and the devotional spirit, shall come the best preparation for all the active duties of life. By such a habit the heart will be kept in tune for every religious duty, and from its practice will grow such a relish for the services of the prayer-meeting as shall make the more special preparation for its exercises a joy, and not a vexatious burden.

> "More holiness give me,
>   More strivings within;
> More patience in suff'ring,
>   More sorrow for sin;
> More faith in my Saviour.
>   More sense of his care!
> More joy in his service,
>   More purpose in prayer."

CHAPTER V.

THE TOPICS.

But in addition to all this, it will be well to have a topic for each meeting, with reference to which the people as well as the pastor may make especial preparation. It should be our endeavor to make each meeting new, fresh and stimulating; both helpful and hopeful. Prayer-meetings have come to be so proverbially stale and unprofitable, because the excellent brethren who take part week in and year out repeat over and over the same remarks and the same prayers. The daily cultivation of piety will give depth and flavor to prayer and the religious life; and a given topic previously announced will afford the people an opportunity to arrange their thoughts with reference to it, and to select such things from their experience as shall illustrate the topic in an interesting manner and on the principle of unity. When the people assemble in ignorance of the subject and the line of thought to be presented, it is not to be looked for that all parts shall fit into their place, and tend to produce a deep and abiding impression; or, indeed, that they shall speak at all to edification and to the point. Lord Nelson had a carefully prepared plan for the battle of Trafalgar, in which each ship had its place assigned in the line of action, and all together were so massed that they should form a wedge, and sweep right through the ranks of the enemy. As he planned, so it proved. The victory was decisive, and placed him in the front rank of great naval heroes. When the exercises are so arranged that they have plan and unity; when the chapter read, the hymns sung, the remarks made, and the prayers offered are so directed that they illustrate the given topic, and the special needs of the church, each part will take its place in the line to form the wedge, and no one will be able to go away and say the meeting lacked purpose, point and power.

Nor will it be found an easy matter to select just the right kind of topics for the prayer-meeting. It would not be surprising if ministers spent as much time over this as over selecting the subject and text for their sermons. In order to avoid this difficulty and the loss of time many have chosen the topics of the Sunday-school lesson, and made them the basis of their remarks. Much might be said in favor of this; it has the advantage of system and publicity; and so gives opportunity to others beside the minister, to make intelligent remarks upon the subject. Speech, to be most profitable needs to be premeditated as to the substance of thought. Where both words and thought are extempore, unless the man is inspired for the occasion, it will be just as well if he kept silent. There is one part, being all unstudied, that requires no preparation—" you may do it extempore," for it is nothing but roaring, and though he "aggravate his voice," and roar as gently as the dove, or " 'twere any nightingale," in the prayer-meeting, it is out of place, and will hardly do any man's heart good or tend to edification.

But the Sunday-school topics are selected more with reference to the wants of a school than the needs of a prayer-meeting and daily Christian life. If there is a general attendance on the prayer-meeting and the Sunday-school—as is desirable—it takes away from the freshness of the theme, and the interest in it also, to have the same topic presented twice, and, in connection with the teachers' meeting, thrice in the same week. The topics more especially needed for the week-day meeting are such as grow out of the trials and burdens of daily life, and should be so adapted to them as to confer sympathy, bestow strength and patience, and promote growth in grace. The prayer-meeting should give scope for such themes as are particularly adapted to edify the body of Christ, to confirm faith, to quicken love, to illustrate doctrine, and to stimulate life in its various fields of useful labor. Hence the more appropriate themes are such as make plain our duty to God, to self, and to fellow-man. The topics should be selected with reference to the guidance of experience along "the path of the just," which "is as the shining light, that shineth more and more unto the perfect day."

And topics might also be selected occasionally to bear some relevancy to the progress of time and the changing seasons. Thus, for a New Year's week we might have a dedication service, on some such theme as this, "Choose ye this day whom ye will serve," or "Mary's Choice," Luke 10: 38-42. For a Spring service we might choose a topic like this, "Seed Time," Gal. 6: 7; or we might arrange for a "Floral Service," just as Spring is passing into Summer, and is now standing in its pride and glory—"Consider the lilies of the field, how they grow," Matt. 6: 28. "A study on flowers" of this kind would teach valuable lessons as well as give suitable opportunity to pray for a blessing upon the sowing of the seed and the increase of the material harvest in its season. A promise meeting might be arranged for some time during the progress of Summer, and opportunity given for rehearsing the promises of God and their unfailing fulfilment in our experience. "A harvest festival" would be appropriate for the Autumn and the ingathering of grain and fruit. These would find their counterpart in the garniture of life's spiritual harvest, 2 Cor. 9: 6, and Gal. 6: 8. Themes kindred to this would be, "The Summer is ended," "Fruits meet for repentance," "The fruit of the Holy Spirit," or "The fruit of the lips." And on Thanksgiving week it would be very appropriate to have a general praise meeting, in which the people may express what they have to be thankful for; and such a meeting on their part would prove a most excellent preparation for the public observance of the Day of Thanksgiving. And for the close of the year we might have a remembrance meeting, "Hitherto hath the Lord helped us," 1 Sam. 7: 12. It would be very profitable to review the signal providences of the year, and apply the teachings of age to renewed fidelity; for time is short and its flight rapid. Would not such a meeting as this deepen our appreciation of the 90th psalm, and especially that devout petition, "So teach us to remember our days that we may apply our hearts unto wisdom!" Topic would suggest topic as the seasons come and go, and in this way we could appropriately arrange for evenings in which to illustrate the various teachings of nature as they bear upon life. We should find occasions in this way to use the great phenomena of nature, and use them as the Bible uses them, to illustrate life and its meanings. In this way mountain, river, sea, storm, wind, rain, dew, ice and snow could be used for the topics at such times as would render them appropriate, but not so frequently as to destroy freshness and render their teachings " stale and unprofitable."

And this matter of set topics has already had the trial of years and has been found most expedient by those churches which have used them. There is before me among others the list that was used by the Second Presbyterian Church of Indianapolis, Ind., during the last year of the pastorate of Dr. J. L. Withrow. We insert it at the close of this chapter, both to commend the method and to show the nature of the topics, that in this way our hints may have the benefit of example as well as precept.

TOPICS.

Date	Topic	Reference
Jan. 6.	Daily Benefits,	Psalms 68 : 19
13.	Suffering due to Sin,	John 5 : 5
20.	Refusing and the Results,	John 5 : 40
27.	Born Again,	John 3 : 3
Feb. 3.	Evidences of Sonship.	Rom. 8 : 14
10.	Resist the Devil,	James 4 : 7
17.	Meaning of	Col. 2 : 10
24.	Retribution,	Rom. 2 : 6
Mar. 2.	Sparing Begets Sparseness,	2 Cor. 9 : 6

Mar. 9.	Lying,	Col. 3 : 9
16.	God Forgetting Sins,	Heb. 10 : 17
23.	Christ in Providence,	Heb. 1 : 3
30.	Number of the Blest Unknown,	Matt. 14 : 14
April 6.	Inspiration of the Scriptures,	2 Tim. 3 : 16
13.	Searching the Scriptures,	John 5 : 39
20.	Meaning of	Hab. 2 : 4
27.	Cleansing Blood,	1 John 1 : 7
May 4.	The good times of the Ungodly,	Psalms 73 : 5
11.	Christ, the Leader,	Is. 55 : 4
18.	The Intercessor,	Heb. 7 : 25
25.	Believing all the Bible,	John 5 : 47
June 1.	Union of Faith and Everlasting Life,	John 6 : 47
8.	Faith Kneeling at His Feet,	John 11 : 32
15.	How?	2 Cor. 5 : 21
22.	Meaning of Repentance,	Acts 2 : 38
29.	Sublimity of Unselfishness,	2 Cor. 12 : 15
July 6.	Genuine Love,	1 John 3 : 18
13.	The Sin Bearer,	1 Peter 2 : 24
20.	Believing vs. Working,	Rom. 4 : 5
27.	The Living Fountain,	Rev. 7 : 17
Aug. 3.	Evils of Indulgence,	1 Cor. 9 : 25
10.	Refuge from Storm,	Is. 25 : 4
17.	Friend of Friends,	Prov. 18 : 24
24.	Explain	Rom. 6 : 1
31.	Saved by Hope,	Rom. 8 : 24
Sept. 7.	Putting on Christ,	Rom. 13 : 14
14.	Safety,	Psalms 91 : 1
21.	All-Seeing Eye,	Prov. 15 : 3
28.	Full Satisfaction,	Psalms 17 : 15
Oct. 5.	In what Sense?	Rom. 6 : 18
12.	Foolishness of Preaching,	1 Cor. 1 : 18
19.	Better than he Asked,	2 Cor. 12 : 9
26.	Crowned with many Crowns,	Rev. 19 : 12
Nov. 2.	Consulting Others' Weakness,	Rom. 15 : 1
9.	Relation of Believers to the Saviour,	Col. 2 : 7
16.	Right kind of Righteousness,	Phil. 3 : 9
23.	Thanksgiving,	Eph. 5 : 20
30.	Harmonize,	Gal. 6 : 2 with 6 : 5
Dec. 7.	Gracious Promise,	Mal. 4 : 2
14.	The Unborn Herald,	Mal. 4 : 5
21.	The Star,	Matt. 2 : 10
28.	The End,	Psalms 39 : 4

CHAPTER VI.

THE TOPICS ILLUSTRATED.

It will prove quite stimulating, and an aid to the fuller understanding of Scriptural truth, to draw from the Bible suitable illustrations of the changing seasons, and of striking events in the history of our church, our community, our state, or our land, as these are providentially unfolded. A few examples have been selected as hints in this direction.

I. The Opening of the Year.
(Luke 13 : 9).

In countries where the vine is cultivated, not by a few wealthy proprietors with a view to an export trade, but by each family on a small scale, with a view to the food of the household, to plant some trees of other kinds within the same enclosure is the rule rather than the exception.* Within this favored spot the owner is willing to make room for one or more fig-trees, for the sake of the fruit, which in such favorable circumstances he expects them to bear.

When the tree had reached maturity, the owner

expected that it should bear fruit; but that year, the next, and the third it continued barren. Having waited a reasonable time, he gave orders that it should be destroyed.

The dresser of the vineyard, as is quite natural, has become attached to the tree, and when the sentence is pronounced against it, a sentiment akin to compassion springs up. " Woodman, spare that tree," is a species of intercession thoroughly natural and human. A very significant exemplification of this parable is found in an Arabian receipt for curing a palm-tree of barrenness: " Thou must take a hatchet, and go to the tree with a friend, unto whom thou sayest, I will cut down the tree, for it is unfruitful. He answers: Do not so, this year it will certainly bear. But the other says, It must needs be—it must be hewn down; and gives the stem of the tree blows with the back of the hatchet. His friend restrains him, crying, Nay, do it not, thou wilt certainly have fruit from it this year; only have patience, and be not over hasty in cutting it down; if it still refuses to bear fruit, then cut it down."

The lesson of this parable is easily read; and when read, it is unspeakably solemn and tender. God is the owner of the vineyard and the fig-tree within its walls. Abraham's seed, natural and mystical, are the fig-tree; and the Mediator between God and man is the dresser of the vineyard, the intercessor for the barren tree. The essential circumstances involved in the fact that the fig-tree grew within the vineyard are: that in soil, south exposure, care and defence, it was placed in the best possible position for bearing fruit. The one fact that it was planted in the vineyard indicates, and was obviously intended to indicate, that the owner had done the best for his fig-tree.

The three kinds of works whereof Scripture speaks may all be illustrated from this parable: First, good works (John 6:28; Tit. 2:7), when the tree having been made good, bears fruit after its own kind; then dead works (Heb. 9:14; Gal. 2:16), such as have a fair outward appearance, but are not the genuine outgrowth of the renewed man—fruit as it were fastened on externally, alms given that they may be gloried in, prayers made that they may be seen; and lastly, wicked works (1 John 3:12; Rom. 13:12; Gal. 5:19), when the corrupt tree bears fruit manifestly after its own kind. Here it is those good fruits that are sought, but of which none are found. And on that command, "Cut it down," St. Basil beautifully bids us note the love which breathes, even in the threatenings of God. "This," he says, "is peculiar to the clemency of God toward men, that He does not bring in punishments silently or secretly; but by His threatenings first proclaims them to be at hand, thus inviting sinners to repentance." That grand old proverb, which so finely expresses the noiseless approach of the divine judgments: "The gods have feet of wool," true for others, is not true for those who have a listening ear. Before the hewing down begins, the axe is laid at the root of the tree.

Christ, as the great Intercessor, pleads for men, yet not that they may always continue unpunished in their sins, but only that their sentence may for a while be suspended; so to prove whether they will turn and repent. The means of grace shall be multiplied, which is so often granted to men and nations in the last period of their probation, and just before those means are withdrawn from them forever. Thus before the flood they had Noah, before the great catastrophes of the Jewish people some of their most eminent prophets, and before its final doom, the ministry of Christ and of His Apostles. This last is intended here; that richer supply of grace, that freer outpouring of the Spirit, which should follow on the death, resurrection and ascension of the Lord. So Theophylact: "Though they were not made better by the law and the prophets, nor yielded fruit or repentance, yet I will water them by my doctrines and passion; it may be that they will then yield fruits of obedience." To us entering upon a new year the door of repentance and improvement is left open still: "If it bear fruit, well. If not, how shall we escape, if we neglect so great salvation?"

—Adapted from Arnot and Trench.

II. Seed-time. *The Sower, the Seed and the Soil.*
(Matt. 13: 1-10).

This parable represents the reception of the Word of God in the world, and presents the causes of failure, and the requirements that are necessary in order to secure an abundant and fruitful harvest.

The causes of failure are:

1. There is a want of spiritual perception. Some of the seed fell by the wayside. There are persons whose religion is all outside—it never penetrates beyond the intellect. Duty is recognized in word—not felt. They are regular at church, understand the catechism and articles, consider the church a most venerable institution, have a respect for religion, but it never stirs the deeps of their being. They feel nothing in it beyond a safeguard for the decencies and respectabilities of social life. Truth of life is subject to failure in such hearts, because it is trodden

down. Wheat dropped by a harvest-cart upon a road, lies outside. There comes a passenger's foot and crushes some of it; then wheels come by,—the wheel of traffic and the wheel of pleasure,—crushing it grain by grain. And again, the seed finding no lodgement, disappears. The fowls of the air come and devour it. This is the picture, not of thought crushed by degrees, but of thought dissipated, and no man can tell when or how it went.

2. There is want of depth in character. Some fell on stony ground, that is, into a thin layer of soil upon a bed of rock. Shallow soil is like superficial character. You meet such persons in life. There is nothing deep about them; it is all on the surface. The superficial servant's work is done, but not thoroughly—lazily, partially.

The superficial workman's labor will not bear inspection. The very dress of such persons betrays the incomplete character of their minds. With such, religion shares the fate of everything else—it is taken up in a superficial way. The seed sprang up quickly; and then withered away as quickly, because it had no depth of root. There are easily moved susceptibilities that play upon the surface of the soul, and then as rapidly pass away. In such persons words are ever at command—voluble and impassioned words. Such a man came to the Master,—running, kneeling, full of warm expressions, engaging gestures, and professed admiration,—he was ready for anything. Well, go sell what thou hast. If you wish to know what hollowness and heartlessness are, you must seek for them in the world of light, elegant, superficial fashion, where frivolity has turned the heart into a rock-bed of selfishness.

3. Impressions come to nothing when the mind is subjected to dissipating influences and yields to them. There is nutriment in the ground for thorns, and enough for wheat; but not enough in any ground for both wheat and thorns. The heart has a certain power of loving, but love, dissipated on many objects, concentrates itself on none. God *or* the world, not both. "No man can serve two masters." "If any man love the world, the love of the Father is not in him." "The cares of this world, and the deceitfulness of riches, choke the word!" There is a way God has of dealing with such, which is no pleasant thing to bear. In agriculture it is called *weeding*, and in gardening it is done by *pruning*.

In the second place, the permanence of religious impressions requires three things:

1. An honest and good heart is indispensable. Earnestness is necessary for real success in everything.

The miser sacrifices all to his single passion; hoards the pennies and dies possessed of wealth. Time and pains will do anything. "The kingdom of heaven suffereth violence, and the violent take it by force." Sow for time, and *probably* you will succeed in time. Sow the seed of Life,—humbleness, pure-heartedness, love,—and in the long eternity which lies before the soul, every minutest grain will come up again with an increase of thirty, sixty, or an hundred fold.

2. Meditation is necessary. They keep the word which they have heard. In meditation on religious truth, if it be first loved, it will recur spontaneously to the heart. And as it is dwelt on, it receives innumerable applications; is again and again brought up to the sun and tried in various lights, and so incorporates itself with the realities of practical existence. Meditation is done in silence. By it we renounce our narrow individuality, and expatiate into that which is infinite. There is a divine depth in silence—we meet God alone.

3. Endurance likewise is necessary. "They bring forth fruit with patience." The patience for us to cultivate is to bear and to persevere. However dark and profitless, however painful and weary existence may have become; however any man, like Elijah, may be tempted to cast himself beneath the

juniper-tree and say, "It is enough: now, O Lord!" Life is not done, and our Christian character is not won, so long as God has anything left for us to suffer, or anything left for us to do. Patience is also opposed to that restlessness which cannot wait. This is one of the difficulties of spiritual life. We are disappointed if the harvest do not come at once.

From all this it is evident that the causes of failure cannot be attributed to the seed nor to the sower, but entirely to the soil.

> " Let us, then, be up and doing,
> With a heart for any fate;
> Still achieving, still pursuing,
> Learn to labor and to wait."
>
> —*Selected and abridged from Robertson.*

III. A Summer Service. The Lesson of Flowers.
(Matt. 6 : 28).

We are now almost midway in the season of flowers, between the coming of the early violet and the late chrysanthemum, and are witnessing them in their various phases of bloom, beauty, glory, and rapid decay. Material things are the visible and transient forms into which ideas have been cast, and a flower forms one of the many words which God uses in the language of symbolism for lessons of truth and wisdom. We are too apt to think that the material things of earth alone have permanence and reality, and serve as the patterns of all thinking and experience, but this is the error of materialism. The truth is on the other side. The pattern of things is unseen and eternal. Thoughts are not the fleeting shadows which matter casts; but more correctly matter in its various forms is their shadow (2 Cor. 4:18; Col. 2:17; Heb. 8:5; and 9:23). What, then, are some of the lessons which flowers teach?

1. From time immemorial the gift of a flower has conveyed the language of esteem and friendship, and in their use on Decoration Day they have come to be emblematical of the affection entertained for those who gave their lives to the service of their country. Flowers form the symbolism of love and beauty, as appears from such popular names as "forget-me-not," "love-lies-bleeding," etc. And in a sick room they are there with their fragrance and beauty to remind the sick of the love we cherish for them, and silently to preach of a beauty that fades not like their own—immortal in the skies.

2. Their color, beauty and fragrance command attention and are unrivalled. Christ called himself "The Rose of Sharon and the Lily of the Vallies." (Cant. 2:1). The flowers of the field were intro-

duced into the Sermon on the Mount to illustrate a variety of truths. Consider: Solomon in all his glory was not arrayed like one of these.

3. Their perfectibility. The breath of sin, the blast of winter and the mildew of death fell upon them when they were plucked out of Paradise and scattered over the earth. That they suffered deterioration is evident from the fact that kindly culture has so greatly improved their bloom and multiplied their variety. Flowers come to us from the paradise that is past to tell us of a lost and faded beauty, and to prophesy of a greater and grander beauty that shall not, like their own, so soon pass away. Music is another language of sentiment and emotion, which seems to have come down to us from the paradise above—a wave of melody that has burst through the gates of heaven and overflowed its walls, that our souls might be thrilled with the harmonies of the endless life and the heavenly bliss, where God is praised with unsinning hearts. Flowers and music tell us of the "Paradise Lost" and the "Paradise Regained," and prophesy of the beauty and harmony that shall yet prove unending.

4. We are also to learn from flowers the shortness of life and the corruptibility of all earthly glory. Walk through the field in its beauty and fragrance of

grass and flower. The glory of spring soon passes into summer and fades away into the tints of autumn; or wither and die under the scorching heat of the sun and the fiery blast, and it is all gone. David as he tended his father's flocks had been impressed by it, and when he wrote the 103d Psalm he remembered it and said, the life of man is just like this. Like the grass and flowers of the field, so he flourishes and so he departs. (Ps. 103 : 15, 16; also, Is. 40: 6-8, and 1 Peter 1 : 24).

5. The rose is a sign of fertility. (Is. 35 : 1).

6. Flowers preach a most impressive sermon on Providence.

> What a world of thought and care
> Makes the tiny flower fair!

Destined to bloom for a day; if God is so lavish here, how much more shall not His love and care extend to His creatures who have sentient life and are capable of loving Him. (Matt. 6 : 28-34). What a lesson is here for the man that is fearful and desponding—that is lacking in faith and hope. He ought to read this lesson every day. God will not and does not forget. If He take care of birds and flowers, how much more will his thoughts extend to you, O ye of little faith!

7. But life in its unfoldings here is so short—why

should we grieve if we are subject to its harsh mutations. There is nothing that more keenly tries character than the sudden gain or loss of wealth. By that the poor man's head is oft made giddy; by this the rich man's heart is crushed, and his hope and ambition fly away with his riches. But why should it be so? Life is like the flower of the grass; mutation is its order. And besides we are tried thus sorely, in order that character—the perpetual and enduring fruit of the flower— may become firm and noble, and may not be unhinged by these severe blasts that sweep over it. Prosperity like adversity soon passes away, and these distinctions perish in the tomb. But what if he should miss the crown of life? "Blessed is the man that endureth temptation: for when he is tried, he shall receive the crown of life, which the Lord hath promised to them that love him." (Jas. 1: 8–12.)

—*By the writer, from the* INTERIOR.

IV. *A Topic for Autumn.*

"We all do fade as a leaf." (ISA. 64: 6.)

In the late autumn days, the saddest of the year, Nature is preaching to us a solemn sermon from the most solemn of all texts. This lesson is whispered by every bleak wind that moans through the waning wood; it is proclaimed in melancholy murmurs by every stream that wanders through the valley, choked with the relics of former beauty and luxuriance; it is painted in brown and sombre hues on every part of the landscape. The burden of every sound we hear, the moral of every sight we see, is the old, old truth, which finds a ready response in every human bosom, " We all do fade as a leaf."

Leaves are beautiful objects—rich in color, graceful in shape, simple in structure—they are among the most exquisite productions of Nature's loom.

1. Leaves fade gradually. The whole foliage of a tree does not fade and pass away at once. Some leaves droop and wither even in Spring, when the rest of the foliage is in its brightest and most luxuriant beauty. Some are torn away in summer, while green and full of sap, by sudden and violent storms. The great majority fade and fall in autumn; while a few cling to the branches all through the cold and desolation of winter, and are at last pushed off by the unfolding buds of the following spring. And is it not so with every human generation? Generation after generation will come and go; tree after tree will fall and perish; forest after forest will disappear; and thus it will continue until the cycle of man's existence on earth be complete, and the angel shall come, and

swear that Time shall be no longer, and death itself shall die.

2. Leaves fade silently. As He veiled His wondrous working for the Israelites at the Red Sea with the cloud of night, and the dawn only revealed the complete miracle, so in the field of nature, He reveals to us not processes, but results. One by one the leaves become discolored and drop off; but we cannot trace the insidious progress of the blight from its commencement to its consummation, and the first notice we have of the change is the hectic hue upon their surface. Who is to be the first to receive the message to pass hence—we know not; an awful uncertainty rests upon that. The veil that hides it from our view is woven by the hand of mercy. But certain it is that some must go first. The process of decay has begun in some already.

"Leaves have their time to fall;
  And flowers to wither at the north wind's breath:
But thou *all* seasons—all;
  Thou hast all seasons for thine own, O death!
We know when moons shall wane,
  When summer birds from far shall cross the sea,
When autumn leaves shall tinge the golden grain:
  But who shall teach us when to look for thee!"

3. Leaves fade differently. The autumnal foliage is very varied. They all presented a uniform green-

ness in summer; but decay brings out their individual character, and shows each of them in its true colors. When death comes, the true character of each person is made apparent. Precious in the sight of the Lord is the death of His saints; precious and also beautiful. "Let me die the death of the righteous, and let my last end be like his."

4. Leaves fade characteristically. The foliage that is gloomiest in its unfolding is most unsightly in its decay; and the leaves that have the richest and tenderest shade of green in April, have the most brilliant rainbow hues in October. And so it is with man: he dies as he lives. A life of godliness ends in a saintly death; and a career of worldliness and sin terminates in impenitence and despair. The law of life is, that the fruit shall be as the seed, and the end as the beginning: unless, indeed, the higher law of divine mercy interposes on a timely repentance. And as the fading itself is characteristic, so also are the results.

5. Leaves fade preparedly. No leaf falls from the tree—unless wrenched off suddenly and unexpectedly in early growth by external violence—without making due preparation for its departure. Go to the forest or the field, and examine every tree or flower in this sad season of decay, and you will find to your

surprise and delight that "there is as much of life as of death in autumn"—that the elements of future resuscitation and growth are provided for, amid tokens of universal decadence and corruption. Already "another year is hidden along the bough." As surely as the leaf fades so shall we fade. We may imagine it distant. A thousand unforeseen foes, fatal to life, line our path on either side, and we have to run the gauntlet daily between them. We began to die the moment we began to live. Our very life itself is nothing else but a succession of dying; and every day and every hour, in the changes within and without which we experience, wears away a part of it. Should we not then so count our days that we may apply our hearts to heavenly wisdom?—the wisdom of knowing, and loving, and serving Him who alone can redeem our poor perishing life from its vanity, and change it into the glory and blessedness of a life hid with Christ in God. Apart from Him, the industry of a lifetime is but elaborate trifling, "the costly embroidering of a shroud." United to Him our labor is not in vain in the Lord, our works shall endure and follow us. Every leaf on the tree of humanity must fade; but if we are grafted by a living faith in Him whose name is the "Branch," His own gracious promise becomes a living truth to us: "I am the resurrection and the life: he that believeth in Me, though he were dead, yet shall he live; and whosoever liveth, and believeth in Me, shall never die."

> "On the tree of life eternal,
> Man, let all thy hopes be stayed,
> Which, alone forever vernal,
> Bears a leaf which shall not fade."

—Abridged from BIBLE TEACHINGS IN NATURE.

CHAPTER VII.

ONE METHOD FOR THE SELECTION OF TOPICS.

I gladly avail myself at this place of some judicious remarks on the selection of topics, and insert them here for their permanent value, which were first written for the *Interior* by the Rev. J. C. McClintock, of Burlington, Iowa, and printed in that paper last year, under the caption " Themes from the Pews." A method like this, in the absence of uniform topics, or the continuous study of the Scriptures, seems well calculated to wake up the mind of the people, and lead them to take a deeper interest in the prayer-meeting and its spiritual improvement.

"n her delightfully suggestive article, Mrs. Cooper wonders what sort of themes we preachers would talk upon if the pews gave them to us. I have wondered, too; and I have often feared that we missed the very subjects, sometimes, that our people most needed. We, sitting in our studies, do not always get into full sympathy with the daily life of our people. We come to them with a sermon about the philosophy of religion, and they have come to us to hear how to be patient when the children are cross, and submissive to Providence when business is going all wrong.

I determined to try the experiment of letting the people select the themes that we would talk about in prayer-meeting, and to see if in this way I could not get a little nearer to their every-day life and wants. So I quietly asked a number of people, representing the various classes in my church, to prepare a list of ten or fifteen subjects, such as they would like to have explained and prayed over, and hand them to me. I had a splendid response. To be sure, the topics did not differ from those I would have chosen, as much as I supposed; and I was glad of it. For it encouraged me to think that the pulpit and the pews did understand each other pretty well after all. But the topics were fresh; the passages of Scripture chosen to illustrate them were very well selected, and I felt sure the people who made the selection would be interested in the study of their own topics. Out of the seventy or eighty handed to me by different persons, there were enough duplicates to cut down the total to about the number needed for a year. I arranged those—and it was interesting to note how they covered nearly the whole range of Christian experience, daily life, and vital doctrine, and then I had them printed in neat shape and given to everybody in the congregation.

We had such topics as: "The Helping Hand," Gal. 6: 1-10; "Out into the Highways," Luke 14: 16-24; "The Daily Walk," Eph. 5: 1-21; "Relationship to Christ," Matt. 12: 46-50; "Christ's Sympathy," John 11: 21-44; "My Duty to the Prayer-meeting," Heb. 10: 19-29; "Christ's Death for Sin," Is. 53: 1-12; "The Coming of Christ," Matt. 24: 37-51; "Planning our Business," James 4: 13-17; "Honesty in all Things," Prov. 20: 10-23; "How to be Saved," John 3: 14-21; "The World for Christ," Ps. 2: 1-12.

The result was so pleasing and profitable in every way, that I have continued the plan. I am sure it has been a help to me, and a great benefit to the people and the prayer-meeting.

Why might not our churches generally unite on some such list of topics for the prayer-meeting, and get the help that comes from united effort and prayer, even as we have in the Sunday-school? Some time since, a correspondent proposed this in your columns. I don't know who it was, but I would like to shake his hand."

CHAPTER VIII.

THE BIBLE AND THE TOPICS.

Is is our main design to present a variety of ways in which the prayer-meeting may be conducted to interest and edification. A great object will be gained if we can secure a united and continuous study of the Bible. "Search the Scriptures, for in them ye think ye have eternal life, and they are they which testify of me." This can doubtless be secured by selecting some book of the Bible, and letting a paragraph or a section of it suggest the themes to be considered in the prayer-meeting from week to week until the book is finished. This method is at present being followed by the Third Presbyterian Church of Chicago, Dr. A. E. Kittredge, pastor. Just now, as we learn, they are considering the Gospel of St. John. It is scarcely necessary to say that the prayer-meeting of this church is well known for its continued interest, and a weekly attendance of from four to six hundred persons the year around. It would be well if, as in their case, the people were supplied with copies of the Bible at the prayer-meeting, to follow the reading and its exposition, or to take part in the reading whenever that is desirable. In fact the "Bible Reading" of our day is emphasizing the importance of the people having copies of the Bible with them in all religious meetings, that they may acquire readiness in turning from book to book and chapter to chapter in search of Scriptural truth or expositions of it, as well as acquire familiarity in the use of the Bible and become mighty in the Scriptures. In this way the truth will pass to the heart, not only through the ear, but also through the eye, and such assistance will prove valuable; for the greater the number of senses we can employ in bringing home the truth, the deeper will be its impressions, and the more lasting its influence.

This method has its peculiar advantages that recommend it in the absence of any plan that has been systematized, with reference to a full knowledge of Bible doctrine in its applications to daily needs and a steady growth in grace. It has all the advantages of expository preaching. Rev. F. W. Robertson, soon after entering upon his ministry at Trinity Chapel, Brighton, announced his intention of expounding different books of the Bible on Sunday afternoons that he might secure for himself greater freedom, both in subject and in style, than the sermon afforded. In this way he went through First and Second Samuel, the Acts, Genesis, and the Epistles to the Corinthians. In Samuel he was permitted to expound " Hebrew national life, and, incidentally, the experiences of particular individuals of that nation,— in all of which he discerned lessons for the English people, and for the men and women who sat before him. Thus it occurred that topics of national policy, so far as bearing on individuals,—questions of social life—of morals, as they are connected with every-day life, arose naturally, and were treated with unshrinking faithfulness." And the Epistles to the Corinthians were selected more particularly, " because they afford the largest scope for the consideration of a great variety of questions in Christian casuistry, which he thought it important to be rightly understood."

By this method, too, a very large portion of inspired truth will be presented at each meeting. The subjects considered will grow out of the chapters themselves, and will have such progressive movement in thought, variety, and unity, as the book itself possesses. In this way truths that might otherwise be overlooked will receive proper and needful attention, and the greater variety of subjects thus considered will do much to relieve the successive meetings, either from being too disjointed, or from being mere repetitions of the same lines of thought. "Preachers," it has been well said, "are too apt to get the truth before their congregations, in one way only—whatever one they find they have the greatest facility for; and that is like playing on one chord—men get tired of the monotony. Whereas, preaching should be directed to every element of human nature that God has implanted in us—to the imaginative, to the highly spiritual, to the moral, to that phase of the intellectual that works up and toward the invisible, and to the intellectual, that works down to the material and tangible."

And in addition to all this, it may give opportunity to handle certain subjects that may be particularly needed in the way of rebuke, correction, or exhortation, without giving offence, or permitting it to be said that the subjects in question had been selected with particular reference to "hitting certain persons" in the church.

And finally, we will name a small number of books to be used in connection with this method, and in fact with all study of the Bible, which will form in itself a valuable library, or at least lay the foundation for one, in the Christian household. These are: the

THE PRAYER-MEETING. 73

Bible, a Bible Text-Book, a Concordance, a Dictionary of the Bible, a Bible Commentary, a Harmony of the Gospels, a History of the Church, an Atlas of Bible Lands, a History of Doctrines, a History of the World, and Webster's Dictionary Unabridged.

And as an addition to this chapter, though not intimately connected with it, we will give two illustrations to show how geography and chronology may be made the handmaids of Bible history, and serve as "eyes" to the fuller understanding of scriptural truth.

"The physical and general geographical features of the Holy Land should be fully comprehended. Palestine proper is but a small country—not as large as Maryland and Delaware. The plan we suggest is that a few of the most prominent places, representing the various parts of the land, be selected and fixed indelibly on the memory. Their physical peculiarities, their distance and direction, say from Jerusalem, and some historical event for which they were each noted, might be studied, and this would help to give them distinctness. Let us take a few places as, follows: Beersheba, forty-two miles north-west of Jerusalem, the old home of the patriarchs, on the borders of the desert; Hebron, sixteen miles south of Jerusalem, here Abraham purchased the cave of Macpelah; Samaria, thirty-eight miles north of Jerusalem, capital of the kingdom of Israel, with its wicked kings; Capernaum, eighty-one miles north of Jerusalem, the scene of so many of our Lord's miracles and discourses; Dan, one hundred and nine miles north of Jerusalem, on the northern extremity of Palestine, here Jereboam set up the golden calf; Tyre, one hundred and six miles north of Jerusalem, the great commercial city of antiquity; Acre, eighty miles north-west of Jerusalem, 'the key of Syria,' famed in many a war; Joppa, thirty-five miles westward from Jerusalem and the port of that city; and Ramoth-Gilead, forty miles northeast of Jerusalem, one of the cities of refuge, and the place where King Ahab was slain. If these leading points are imprinted permanently on the memory, and all scriptural incidents associated with one or the other of them or with Jerusalem, then an important key has been furnished for opening the sacred treasury.

God has seen fit to convey the knowledge of his will to us largely through history. Accordingly in the Bible we have the history of the way in which salvation was wrought out for mankind, of God's providential dealings with both good and bad men, of the condition of the race when its Creator was discarded, and of the world both with and without religion. We would suggest the following outline for sacred history:

EPOCH.	B. C.	NAME OF PERIOD.	Length of Period.
1. Creation................	4004		
2. Deluge.................	2348	Antediluvian Period............	1656
3. Call of Abraham........	1921	Noachian Period...............	427
4. Descent into Egypt.....	1706	Patriarchal Period	215
5. Exodus.................	1491	Egyptian Period................	215
6. Passage of the Jordan..	1451	Wilderness Period..............	40
7. Establishment of the Monarchy...........	1095	Period of the Judges...	356
8. Division of the Monarchy	975	Period of United Monarchy....	120
9. Capture of Jerusalem...	587	Period of Divided Monarchy...	388
10. Close of Old Testament History............	397	Period of the Captivity.........	190
11. Birth of Christ.........	00	Period of the World Powers...	397

These divisions of time have been made with especial reference to the history of the Bible. It will take but a very short time to memorize these ten dates, and it is recommended that they be repeated hundreds of times, if necessary, so as to become perfectly indelible and familiar. The assertion is ventured that whoever does this will be astonished and delighted at the assistance it will afford in understanding the Bible history, at the order into which it will reduce the various events, and at the light it will throw over the whole book."

—*Selected from Dr. Murphy.*

CHAPTER IX.

BIBLE READINGS FOR THE PRAYER MEETING.

A praying church will be a Bible-reading church, and a Bible-reading church will be a praying church. Either practice will induce the other. The revival in Bible-reading which is so prominent a feature of the Great Awakening in our day, shows its connection with vital godliness, and the importance to be attached to it as a permanent instrumentality.

A Bible reading* may occasionally be introduced into the prayer-meeting to great advantage, and be made to take the place of the usual remarks. This will be found, if rightly conducted, highly interesting

---

*Valuable assistance will be derived from two books lately issued: "Hints on Bible Readings," by Rev. Jno. C. Hill, and "The Hand-Book of Bible Readings," by H. B. Chamberlain; also, "The Hebraist's Vade Mecum," "Eadie's Analytical Concordance," and "Inglis' Bible Text Encyclopedia." Nearly all the so-called evangelists of our day give much attention to this subject, and their preaching frequently is a Bible reading. And even the pastors are beginning to give much attention to the presentation of Gospel truth through the agency of what is called "Bible Reading." As testimony of this we may name Dr. J. H. Brookes, Dr. A. T. Pierson, Dr. J. H. Vincent, Dr. G. F. Pentecost, Rev. Jno. C. Hill, Rev. W. J. Erdman, Rev. W. S. Rainsford, Rev. H. M. Parsons, Rev. G. A. Hall, Rev. W. F. Crafts, Rev. C. M. Whittelsey, Rev. T. B. Stephenson, and many others.

and profitable. God honors the instrumentality of the Word; "for the Word of God is quick and powerful, and sharper than any two-edged sword, piercing even to the dividing asunder of soul and spirit, and of the joints and marrow, and is a discerner of the thoughts and intents of the heart."— Heb. 4. 12.

To make the exercise a success, however, will require considerable study on the part of the leader; perhaps fully as much time as he gives to the preparation of a sermon. But the time thus devoted to the study of the Bible will amply reward him, and repay him much more than it costs. To read and study the Word of God; to have the very words which the Holy Spirit has inspired,—as not merely the basis of our remarks, but the substance of our remarks, cannot prove other than a great blessing.

In order to prepare for a Bible reading the leader should select some important subject relating to Biblical doctrine, Christian daily life and experience, the cultivation of piety, or the practical duties of religion. Having chosen his theme, let him next turn to his Concordance and hunt up all the Scripture texts that really bear upon his topic. Help in the selection may also be derived from Scripture text-books, "Hitchcock's Analysis of the Bible,"

"Locke's Common-place Book of the Holy Bible," "The Englishman's Hebrew and Chaldee Concordance of the Old Testament," "The Englishman's Greek Concordance of the New Testament," and such other books of a kindred nature as he may have in his possession. He will find it very convenient to copy on separate slips of paper each passage with the book and verse indicated from which it is taken. After he has written out all the passages having chief relevancy to his topic, he will then begin to compare Scripture with Scripture, in order to classify the texts and arrange them under their more appropriate divisions. In this way he will soon discover the harmony of Scriptures, and how forcibly, as well as beautifully, they teach and illustrate his subject. As each text is written in full, and separate from the others, it can easily be changed from place to place until the appropriate place and logical order for all have been discovered, and now he can take a strip of paper and pin each text in its place under its proper head and subdivision. The list of texts is now ready to be numbered 1, 2, 3, etc., in the order of sequence for the public reading. If he finds that he has several texts of like import, he can select the one best adapted to illustrate his subject and make a marginal reference to the others without reading them. And between the texts, if they are pinned somewhat apart, he can jot down in outline such remarks and illustrations as will connect the reading, and give it point and application. It will not be enough to read detached portions of Scripture, for in the rapid presentation of the texts alone, the people might fail to catch their import and relative bearing upon your subject.

Major Whittle has given a very serviceable caution to those who have not as yet had much experience with exercises of this sort, that we do well to heed. "Be careful," he says, "not to make the reading too long. Better to divide your topic into five or six readings, and bring out the Scriptures upon each head to your own satisfaction, than to crowd too many heads into one reading. You will find the instruction thus given more easily apprehended and more carefully retained. The fault with most of us lay workers, who have been uninstructed in the logical presentation of truth, is in the beginning of our work to make our readings too cumbersome. My first Bible reading on 'Faith' contained some sixty scriptural references. Before they were all read the audience were tired, and it was a source of anxiety and difficulty for me to interest them. That same Bible reading for one meeting has now developed into *seven*, given as a course, at seven successive meetings, with seeming interest and appreciation on the part of the people, and pleasure to myself."

If you have adopted a list of topics for the prayer-meeting and running through the year, you can select from this list such subjects, at suitable intervals of time, as seem best adapted for exposition by a Bible reading, and then give to its preparation such study and prayer as shall serve to bring out its truths into boldness and clearness of view.

"The very best of Bible readings are gotten up by hard work," says the Rev. Jno. C. Hill—"searching the Scriptures, many of them are long months in making. In order to make these, you must search the Scriptures daily, and at every turn you will find something new; note it, and save it for future use. A good plan is this: have a lot of large envelopes the size of a note sheet, mark them on one corner with a topic—e. g., *love*, assurance, etc.; arrange these in alphabetical order, and whenever you get an idea, lose no time to note it on a slip and place it in its proper envelope. File away your illustrations in the same way. Scrap-books are not well adapted to this work; too much time is lost in pasting and indexing, and even then time is lost in gathering your material scattered all through the book, while by the envelope system you have *all* your scraps and verses before you at a single glance. The lay evangelists, Moody, Whittle, Cole, Moorehouse, and others, use this method."

But as the people are to take part in this exercise, the references may be read by them in concert from their Bibles; or what will doubtless prove more expeditious, by certain ones in the audience who are good readers, and who, having received each a text numbered on a slip of paper prepared for this purpose, will promptly respond. And in case there should be any delay in the reading, it will be best for the leader to read it himself and not delay the meeting.

There are thus two methods* for reading and studying the Bible.

1. To read it continuously. It would be well if every Christian would read his Bible through once every year. "I never heard of a man," says George Rodgers, "who read it right through, and then said he did not believe in it. Read it all through and it will be sure to get hold of you somewhere; it will then get

---

*These methods may be particularized as follows: 1. Reading the word: (a) Daily devotional reading. (b) Social reading. (c) Reading sacred biographies. (d) A book at a continuous reading. 2. Studying: (a) By topics. (b) By words. (c) By references. (d) By books.

Presented by H. B. Chamberlain, at a Y. M. C. A. Conference, lately held at Baldwinsville, N. Y.

into the movement and become a necessity for your being; you cannot after that do without it."

2. To read it topically so as to get its collected and entire teaching on a particular subject. Such Bible reading was not possible before the entire volume was completed. During the 1500 years of its composition the Bible was incomplete and not generally accessible; but now that the canon has been closed and printing invented, the book is so multiplied that every person may possess a copy in its completeness, and read and study its pages both connectedly and separately. And besides this, there are various helps to facilitate his study and guide him to a clearer understanding of the truth.

If the minister can succeed in making his church into a sort of Biblical institute for the continuous and the topical study of the Bible, his labors will be greatly blessed both to them and to others, as well as to himself. And if such reading of the Bible, as has just been sketched, be occasionally made the order for the prayer-meeting, it can hardly be doubted that its influence and result shall be felt and seen in all the departments of life and doctrine ; and that the Church, which is the body of Christ, shall be systematically edified, and the unsaved brought to rejoice in the gracious knowledge and experience of the truth.

CHAPTER X.

ILLUSTRATIONS OF BIBLE READINGS.

We have selected a number of Bible readings, which as examples have peculiar relevancy to our subject—the prayer-meeting. For these selections we are mainly indebted to the two books mentioned in a foot-note to the last chapter.

I. THE HOLY SPIRIT.

1. HIS PERSONALITY.

    He is described in the Word of God as a person, and not as an influence, John 14: 16, 17, 25, 26; 15: 26; 16: 7–15. Acts 8: 29; 10: 19; 15: 28. The words *he* and *him* should always be used, instead of the word *it*, when speaking of the Spirit.

    We are baptized into His name, and He is invoked in prayer, showing that He is a person as truly as the Father and the Son. Matt. 28: 19; 2 Cor. 13: 14; Eph. 6: 18.

    Men are said to vex, to blaspheme, to resist, to grieve, to to quench the Spirit, which they could not do unless He is a person. Isaiah 63: 10; Matt. 12: 31; Acts 7: 51; Eph. 4: 30; 1 Thess. 5: 19.

    He does those things for us that can be done only by a person, for it is He who regenerates, quickens, teaches, reproves, helps and sanctifies the believer. John 3: 5; 6: 63; 16: 8; Rom. 8: 26; 1 Cor. 6: 11.

Personal acts that could not be performed by an attribute or influence are ascribed to Him, as when He is said to know, to reveal, to bestow power, to love, to search the deep things of God, and to distribute of His manifold gifts "to every man severally as He will." John 16: 13, 14; Acts 1: 8; Rom. 15: 30; 1 Cor. 2: 10, 11; 12: 8–11.

It is often affirmed in the Bible that the Spirit "said" and "spake," proving conclusively that He is a person. 2 Sam. 23: 2; Mark 12: 36; Acts 1: 16; 13: 2; 21: 11; 28: 25; 1 Tim. 4: 1; Heb. 3: 7; Rev. 3: 7; 14: 13; 22: 17.

The visible manifestations of the Spirit show that He is a person. Matt. 3: 16; Luke 3: 21, 22; John 1: 32; Acts 2: 3, 4.

2. HIS DIVINITY.

He is called God. 2 Sam. 23: 23; Isa. 6: 8, 9, compared with Acts 18: 25; Jer. 31: 31–34, compared with Heb. 10: 15; Acts 5: 3, 4.

He possesses the perfections of God; as omnipotence, omniscience, omnipresence, holiness, eternal existence, Job 26: 13; Psalm 139: 7; Romans 1: 4; 1 Cor. 2: 10; Heb. 9: 14.

He performs the works of God, Gen. 1: 2; Ex. 31: 3; Job 33: 4; Psa. 104: 30; Isa. 11: 2; Rom. 8: 11; 15: 16, 1 Cor. 2: 14; 2 Peter 1: 21; Rev. 11: 11.

Sin against Him is sin against God. Mark 3: 28, 29: Acts 5: 9; Heb. 4: 7–9; 10: 29.

He exercises the sovereignty and resistless will of God, Num. 9: 26; 24: 2; Jud. 14: 6; 1 Sam. 10: 6; Neh. 9: 20; Isa. 11: 13; Isa. 63: 10, 11, 14; Mic. 2: 7; Zech. 4: 6; Luke 12: 11, 12; Acts 13: 4; 16: 6, 7; 20: 28; 1 Cor. 12: 11.

We depend upon Him as upon God, Mark 13: 11; John 3: 5; 14: 26; 16: 7–14; Acts 4: 31; 9: 31; 10: 19, 20;

Rom. 8: 9–16, 26; 15:13; 1 Cor. 3: 16, 17; 1 John, 4: 13.

We are required to recognize Him as God, Matt. 28 : 19; Rom. 15: 30; 1 Cor. 6:11; 2 Cor. 13:14; Eph. 4:30; 1·John 5:6–9; Rev. 3:22.

3. HE IS REVEALED IN THE OLD TESTAMENT AS FILLING MEN, OR COMING UPON THEM, BUT NOT AS ABIDING WITH THEM, OR DWELLING IN THEM. The Old Testament saints, while saved by the Holy Ghost through faith in the promised Messiah, were not linked to a risen man at God's right hand; but corporately and dispensationally their place was on the earth. Ex. 31:3; Num. 11:25-29; 24:2; Deut. 34:9; Judges 3:10; 6:34; 13:25; 14:6, 19; 15:14; 1 Sam. 10: 6, 10; 11:6; 16:13, 14; 2 Chron. 15:1; 20:14; 24:20; Mic. 3:8; Exodus 19:5, 6; Deuteronomy 32:8; Isaiah 43:9, 10; Amos 3:2.

4. HE IS REVEALED IN THE NEW TESTAMENT AFTER A NEW MANNER AND FOR A NEW PURPOSE, and hence His coming is said to depend upon the finished work of Christ. He is present now in the world to gather out a people unto the name of Jesus, to regenerate them, to abide with them forever, to dwell in them, to sanctify them, to give them their place and portion in the heavens, and to constitute them the body of which the risen Saviour on the right hand of the Majesty on high is the living Head. Acts 15:14; Matt. 3:11; John 3;5; 7:39; 14:16, 17, 26; 15:26; 16:7; Acts 19:2; Rom. 5:5; 8:9; 1 Cor. 6:19; 12:13; Eph. 2:22; 4:4; Hebrews 3:1; 10:34; 1 Peter 1:2; 1 John 4:17.

5. THE PROMISE OF THE COMFORTER WAS FULFILLED ON THE DAY OF OUR LORD'S RESURRECTION, which was also the day of His ascension in behalf of his people; but the promise of the Spirit as the power of testimony and service was fulfilled on the day of Pentecost, following His visible and final ascension to the right hand of God. The same two-fold relation of Christ, first secretly to His own, and then openly in connection

with them to the world at large, runs all through the Scriptures. He comes for His saints, and afterwards appears with them. Compare John 20:22 with Gen. 2:7; John 20:17 with Matt. 28:9; Acts 1:8; 2:1, 17 with Joel 2:23-32. It shows a lack of intelligence for Christians to pray for the Spirit as if He were given occasionally, or as if He had taken His departure; but it is proper to pray for the increased manifestations of His presence and power. John 14:16, 17; Acts 2:33; 4:31; 5:32; 6:5, 8; 7:55; 8:17, 29, 39; 9:31; 10:44; 11:24; 13:2, 4; 15:8; 16:6, 7; 19:6; 20:28; 21:11; Eph. 1:17; Rev. 22:16, 17; Malachi 4:6.

6. THERE IS A STRIKING ANALOGY BETWEEN THE RELATIONS OF THE SPIRITUAL TO THE PERFECT HUMAN NATURE OF CHRIST, AND HIS RELATIONS TO THOSE WHO ARE MADE PARTAKERS OF THE DIVINE NATURE. Christ as a man was born of the Spirit. Matt. 1:18-20; Luke 1:35; Heb. 10:5. He was anointed and sealed with the Spirit. Matt. 3:16; Mark 1:10; Luke 3:22; John 1:32, 33; 6:27; Acts 10:38.

He was led by the Spirit. Matt. 4:1; Mark 1:12; Luke 4:1.
He acted in the power of the Spirit. Matt. 12:28; Luke 4:14-18; John 3:34; Acts 1:2.
He was justified by the Spirit. Romans 1:4; 1 Timothy 3:16.
He offered Himself by the Spirit. Hebrews 9:14.
He was raised up by the Spirit. Romans 8:11; 1 Peter 3:18. See also Isaiah 11:2; Rev. 3:1. So Christians are (a) born of the Spirit. John 3:5, 6, 8; Titus 3:5. (b) They are anointed and sealed with the Spirit, 2 Cor. 1:22; 5:5; Eph. 1:13; 1 John 2:27. (c) They are led by the Spirit, Romans 8:4, 14; 1 Cor. 6:19, 20; Gal. 5:16-18. (d) They act in the power of the Spirit. John 7:38, 39; Acts 1:8; Romans 8:26. (e) They are justified by the Spirit. 1 Cor. 6:11. (f) They offer themselves unto God through the Spirit. Rom. 15:16; 1 Cor. 12:3-13; Galatians 4:4-6; 5:25; 1 Peter 1:2, 22. (g) They are raised up by the Spirit. Romans 8:11.

7. THE OFFICES OF THE SPIRIT IN CONNECTION WITH THE BELIEVER.

He is the Seal. Many think of Him as the Sealer, and are in confusion about the seal; but He Himself is the seal. 2 Cor. 1:22; Eph. 1:13.

He testifies of Christ, and never turns our eyes to the work done in us, but to the work done for us, as the ground of our consolation. John 15:26; 16:14.

He teaches in such a way that the humblest believer who is subject to His guidance is in no need of human authority. John 14:26; 1 Cor. 2:14; 1 John 2:27.

He bears witness by confirming to the heart the truth of God's Word. Romans 8:15, 16; Galatians 4:6; 1 John 5:6.

He dwells in those whom He has united to a risen Christ, and builds them together for an habitation of God. Romans 8:9.; 1 Cor. 6:19.; Eph. 2:22.

He is the author of revelation, and the bestower of all gifts and graces. 2 Pet. 1:21; 1 Cor. 2:10–13; 12:4–11; Gal 5:22, 23.

He is the Comforter and Helper of the saints, and the power of their acceptable worship. John 14:16; Rom. 8:26; Eph. 6:18; Philippians 3:3.; 1 John 3:24; Jude 20. Believers are urged not to grieve or quench the Spirit, while unbelievers are said to resist Him, and their sin is demonstrated by His presence on the earth. Eph. 4:30; 1 Thess. 5:19; Acts 7:51; John 16:8. May we dwell more upon the amazing love of the Spirit, Romans 15:30.

—*Dr. J. H. Brookes.*

Dr. Brookes is the editor of a valuable monthly, THE TRUTH, a publication which contains abundant illustrations of the Word and Bible readings.

II. HOW TO USE THE BIBLE WITH CHRISTIAN WORKERS.

I.—Acquaint yourself with the Bible.

To use the Bible efficiently in your work, you must first be acquainted with it. Jesus says (John 5:39) "*Search* the Scriptures," implying that you must go down beneath the surface to discover the depths of the riches of the wisdom of God. In Acts 17:11 it is written, "These were more noble than those in Thessalonica." Notice the stamp of nobility which God recognizes. Is it nobility of birth? social station? wealth? learning? No! Those were noble men and women, "in that they received the Word with all readiness of mind, and searched the Scriptures daily whether these things were so." That is the title to nobility in God's estimation. Last winter in St. Louis, when the snow was deep, a gentleman on leaving a house one night to enter his sleigh dropped a diamond ring. It sank in the snow. No casual search for it would answer. He at once placed near the spot a large box, hired the policeman to keep search during the night, and at the early dawn made persistent watch until he found it. He did this because it was something precious in his estimation. But what is a diamond compared with the riches of grace and glory which will be found in this blessed book? Seek this acquaintance, because (1) By it we are born again: James 1:18; 1 Peter 1:23. (2) It makes clean: John 15:3. (3) It builds up. Paul says to the elders at Ephesus, "The Word is able to build you up and to give you an inheritance among them which are sanctified." Also, 1 Peter 2:2. (4) It sanctifies and saves. Jesus says (John 17:17), "Sanctify them through thy truth; thy Word is truth." So Paul, 2 Thess. 2:13. (5) It accomplishes God's will: Is. 5:10, 11; Jer. 23:29. (6) It is all powerful: 2 Cor. 10:4. In Ephesians 6:17, the one weapon given for attack upon the foe is the "Sword of the Spirit, which is the Word of God." (7) It is all sufficient, as Jesus declares. Luke 6:31, and in John 5:10-13, we are told "He that believeth not God hath made him a liar." Why? Simply because "he believeth not the record which God gave of his Son."

II.—*All* Scripture is of God: 2 Tim. 3:16. From the first word of Genesis to the last word of Revelation, *all* is inspired: 2 Peter 1:19-21. "We have a more sure word." More sure in one sense than the brightest flashes of glory that were ever seen upon the Mount of Transfiguration. A great many people think prophecy is a dark place. God says here, it is "a light which shines in a dark place." They "spake as they were moved," not as they thought, not as they imagined, but as they were "moved by the Holy Ghost." Hence Jesus in His charge to His disciples, Matt. 10:19, 20, said: "It is not ye that speak, but the Spirit of your Father which speaketh in you." See also Acts 3:21; 4:25; 2 Sam. 23:2.

Moreover the Scripture is called: (1) The oracles of God: Rom. 3:1, 2. (2) The Word of God: Mark 7:13. (3) The Word of the Lord: Acts 8:25. (4) The Word of Truth: 2 Cor. 6:7. (5) The Word of Life: John 6:68. (6) The Word of Christ: Col. 3:16. (7) The Word of Faith: Rom. 10:8, 9.

I want to press this text home upon any unsaved friends. The Word is nigh you to-night; nearer than when St. Paul wrote these verses. An insane woman had shut herself up in a room with a little child till both were nearly dead. When we burst into the room, we found the child lying on the bed able only to whisper, "water, water." When her little trembling hands pressed the goblet to her lips she was scarcely able to hold it; but, as it refreshed her, she seized it with a strong, nervous grasp. When your perishing, thirsty soul receives the word of Faith, not the strength of your grasp on it, but the divine power of the refreshing Word will give consolation and strength.

III.—All Scripture is about Christ: John 5:39-46. He does not say, Search part of them. Again, read Luke 4:21; also Luke 24:25-27. Now observe, that beginning at Moses and *all* the prophets he expounded concerning Himself; Luke 24:32. I do not wonder that their hearts burned within them. Many of the hearts of God's people have burned within them when they have found Christ in the Old Testament, where they never thought of discovering Him before. In Luke 24:44, 45, he says, "*All* things are written there about Me," in those three great divisions of the Old Testament. Look at what is said in Matt. 2: 13–15, in the light of which read Hosea 11:1; Acts 17:2, 3. He did not reason with them out of human science, human logic, or human learning, but out of the Old Testament Scriptures. Remember this when you are attacked as Christian workers by fallible science; and never study the Bible in the light of science, but study science in the light of the Bible. If you want to make efficient workers, build not on a metaphysical basis, but on the divine interpretation of God's blessed Word. Apollos was mighty here; Acts 18:28. In the last chapter of Acts, 23d verse, we see Paul occupied all day with the Old Testament Scriptures. How many of us find enough in the Old Testament to occupy us all day? Mr. Whittle told me last summer of an unlettered man who had studied the Bible until he had become convinced, without any outside suggestions, that the last clause of Rom. 8:1, did not belong there. I believe that man was taught that by the Holy Spirit.

IV.—All Scripture is for ourselves: Rom. 15:4; 1 Cor. 4:2. Believe and act as if you believed that the Word of God is for you; become acquainted with its precious words, and gently lead the lost into the palace of God: 1 Thess. 2:13. The poor empress Carlotta had escaped from the palace. Her physician knew that a rude shock would dethrone forever her tottering reason. Knowing her fondness for flowers, he scattered them in her pathway, and she, charmed like a child, was safely led back again. If you want to become efficient workers for the Master, seek for and strew the beautiful flowers of Scripture in paths of those who have wandered, and lure them back to God.

V.—Cherish as Christian workers a feeling of dependence upon the Holy Spirit. In John 8:38, 39, and Acts 1:8, Jesus inculcates this dependence upon his disciples. In Acts 6:5, Stephen is "full of the Holy Ghost," and in 8th verse, we find him "full of power." We also receive the spirit of adoption: Rom. 8:15, and Gal. 4:6. Until with child-like confidence we know God as our Father, we cannot be efficient workers. Little May Newton three years old, *in her father's arms* fired the explosion which opened Hell Gate to commerce. And the child of God who is filled with His Spirit finds nothing impossible to him : 2 Tim. 1 : 7.

VI.—To become efficient workers, make use of prayer in connection with the Word: Matt. 21 : 21; Luke 11 : 9; John 14 : 13, and 16 : 24. What hath God wrought in answer to prayer? Jas. 5 : 17, 18.

VII.—In your work think of the value of the soul : Matt. 16 : 27; 18 : 10, 11, 14; and of the Lord's approval ; 2 Cor. 5 : 9.

—*Dr. J. H. Brookes.*

III. HOW TO STUDY THE BIBLE.

1. OBJECT IN STUDY.—Find Christ. John 5 : 39; Luke 24 : 27, 44; Acts 28 : 23; 2 Tim. 3 : 16; John 6 : 63; Ps. 138 : 2; John 1 1–14; John 3 : 11–13, 34.

2. LIFE BY THE WORD.—Jas. 1 : 18–21; 1 Pet. 1 : 23; Deut. 8 : 3; John 5 : 39; John 6 : 63; Ps. 119 : 130.

3. GROWTH.—Job 23 : 12; Jer. 15 : 16; John 6 : 35; Matt. 5 : 6; 2 Thess. 2 : 13; Eph. 5 : 26. 1. Pet. 2,2.

4. POWER.—Is. 40 : 8; Ps. 119 : 89; John 15 : 7; Eph. 6 : 17; Heb. 4 : 12; Rom. 10 : 17.

5. SEARCHING IN STUDY.—John 5 : 39; 2 Tim. 2 : 15.

6. DEPENDENCE ON THE HOLY SPIRIT.—John 16 : 13; 15 : 26; Jude 20; Jas. 1 : 5; 1 Cor. 2 : 9, 10, 12, 13.

7. WITH THE WHOLE MIND AND HEART.—1 Chron. 28 : 9; 2 Chron. 15 : 2; Is. 26 : 3.

8. SEEK LIGHT FROM ANY WHO ARE TAUGHT BY THE SPIRIT.—2 Pet. 1 : 20, 21; 1 Tim. 4 : 13–16.

9. AFTER MUCH STUDY HAVE CLEAR, POSITIVE VIEWS.—2 Tim. 1 : 8–13; Ps. 51 : 12, 13.

Pray before reading; read and pray; search and pray; review and pray; hold fast. (2 Tim. 3 : 14–17; 2 Tim. 4 : 7). Look for large results from the right study of the Word of God; for a fuller knowledge of God as Father, Son and Holy Ghost; and for the rich and abundant fruits of the Holy Spirit in daily life. (Gal. 5: 22, 23). —*Selected.*

IV. THE PRAYER OF FAITH.

1. STATE OF HEART.—Helplessness. Matt. 15:25. Need, Matthew 14:30. Want, Acts 16:30. Distance, Luke 18:13. Guilt, Luke 15:21. Condemnation, Ps. 51:4. Defilement, Luke 5:8.

2. LOOKING TO THE LORD.—To Jesus, the Person, Heb. 12:2. The able Saviour, Heb. 7:25. The willing Saviour, Matt. 8:3. The near Saviour, Heb. 10:22. Jesus, our Sacrifice, 1 Cor. 5:7. Jesus, our Substitute, 2 Cor. 5:21. Jesus, our Sanctification, 1 Cor. 1:30.

3. CONFESSION.—Of sin, Ps. 51:3. Of specific sins, 1 John 1:9. Of besetting sins, Heb. 12:1. Of past sins, Ps. 25:7. Of presumptuous sins, Ps. 15:3. Of secret sins, Ps. 19:12.

4. SUPPLICATION.—For pardon, Ps. 51:7. For purity, Ps. 51:10. For the Spirit, Eph. 3:16. For Christ's indwelling, Eph. 3:17, first clause. For knowledge, Eph. 3:19. For saints, Eph. 6:18. For fellowmen, Rom. 10:1.

5. INTERCESSION.—Of the Spirit, Rom. 8:26. For others, 1 Tim. 2:1. For the Word, 2 Thess. 3:1. For the Church, Ps. 122:6. For ministers, Eph. 6:19. In the Spirit, Jude 20. Through Christ, 1 John 2:1, 2.

6. EXPECTATION OF FAITH.—Longing, Ps. 61:1. Promise of help, Ps. 91:14. Promise of deliverance, Ps. 91:15. Promise of comfort, Ps. 60:15. Promise of rest, Matt. 11:28. Promise of gifts, Matt. 7:7. Satisfaction of all desires, Matt. 11:24.

7. IMPORTUNITY.—Constancy, 2 Chron. 15:2, last half. Delight, Ps. 37:5. Complete confidence, Ps. 37:5. Continuance, Luke 18:1; 1 Thess. 5:17. Persistence, Gen. 32:26. Repetition, 2 Cor. 12:8, 9. Assurance, John 15:7.

—*Rev. H. M. Parsons.*

V. WHAT A PRAYER-MEETING SHOULD BE.

1. REGULAR AND PUNCTUAL ATTENDANCE.—Heb. 10 : 25.
2. BRING OTHERS.—Num. 10 : 29.
3. COME PRAYING.—John 12 : 21 ; John 15 : 5.
4. CONTINUE IN PRAYER.—Acts 1 : 4, 14.
5. AVOID CRITICISM.—Ps. 133 : 1 ; Rom. 12 : 10 ; ~~John 17 : 23~~ ;
6. PARTICIPATE PROMPTLY AND HEARTILY IN THE EXERCISES.—Col. 3 : 16 ; 2 Cor. 1 : 11 ; Heb. 4 : 16.
7. LET ALL THE EXERCISES BE BRIEF.—Eccl. 5 : 2.
8. KEEP IN MIND THAT WE SPEAK AND SING BEFORE GOD. —2 Cor. 12 : 19.
9. CHRISTIAN TESTIMONY.—Ps. 40 : 10 ; 51 : 15 ; 63 : 3-5 ; 119 : 171, 172 ; Isa. 43 : 10 ; Mal. 3 : 16, 17 ; Heb. 3 : 13 ; Jas. 5 : 6 ; Matt. 10 : 32, 33 ; John 12 : 42 ; 1 Cor. 1 : 5 ; 2 Cor. 8 : 7 ; Rom. 10 : 9, 10.

—Rev. W. F. Crafts.

CHAPTER XI.

A Plan for Each Meeting.

Those meetings will prove the most refreshing and successful for which both pastor and people have made suitable preparation. And just how to make the meetings successful has been one of the important subjects which the ministerial conventions held in connection with the revival labors of Mr. Moody and Major Whittle have discussed. As a result, the attention of all the churches has been aroused to the importance of the subject, and the matter has been somewhat agitated by the religious press. And the answer to the whole matter is this: if we are to have successful prayer-meetings we must pray, work, and plan for them—in a word have an intelligent plan for each meeting.

"We published last week," says the *Interior*, "some pertinent suggestions by a contributor as helps to prayer-meeting interest. We notice decided progress in the attention everywhere given to the question how to make meetings for prayer more interesting. And pastors and churches are beginning to plan for these meetings as they do for the Sunday-school service or for the Week of Prayer. People used to have an indefinite sort of idea that a prayer-meeting was self-propelling. In some quarters there has been a shrinking from studying and planning for that meeting, as if it implied some lack of reliance on the Holy Spirit. Just so the ranters used to decry pulpit preparation, relying instead on the direct operation of the Spirit. Such blind reliance spoils the sermon.

"We are learning in all church work, he honors God most who is most diligent in the use of all means that tend to success. Therefore, let every method be tried by which the vitality and power of the prayer-meeting may be secured. Let us not be afraid of having a little well-planned machinery, even in a prayer-meeting. The idea that no prayer-meeting is good which is not voluntary and extemporaneous in the character of its exercises, should be discarded. When all hearts are full and minds alert, it will be sufficient to throw the meeting "open," though even then there is always the hazard that it may be spoiled by the very freedom which sometimes leads to highest success.

"But the responsibility for the prayer-meeting and

its right conduct by no means rests with ministers alone. If every church member would hold his duty to be at the prayer-meeting to be as sacred as his business engagements, and being at the meeting, would refuse to be merely a sponge to absorb, but would communicate according to the gift that was in him, the complaint about dry meetings would cease, and the hour of prayer be, as it should be, the most delightful of all the week."

But, perhaps the chief points which a definite plan should include relate to reading of the Scriptures, prayer, remarks, singing, voluntary parts, and the length of the meeting.

1. Reading the Scriptures. The portion to be read for the evening lesson should be selected with care, and especial reference to the illustration of the evening's subject. It is very desirable that the people should follow the reading from their own Bibles, and in this way get into full sympathy with the truth to be presented as early as possible. It is often the case that a meeting does not fully wake up until it is about time to be dismissed; and so it has been remarked, If we could only begin the next meeting in the spirit and the enthusiasm with which this one closed, we should all be ready to sing, speak and pray. Do not slight the reading. The eloquent

McAll is reported to have said: "If the Lord had appointed two officers in His church, the one to preach the Gospel, and the other to read the Scriptures, and had given me the choice of these, I should have chosen to be a reader of the inspired Word of God." And in point of fact there is no part of any religious service that can be slighted with safety. We ought to feel that one part is as important as another, and that God can bless even the minutest particular to the conversion and edification of souls. A venerable minister testified in a clergyman's meeting that one of the most powerful impressions produced on his early life was made by Asahel Nettleton, the noted revivalist, in his reading the hymn,

"Ashamed of Jesus! that dear Friend
On whom my hopes of heaven depend."

The truths of that hymn went home to his heart as nothing in his sermon did. He looked back over fifty years of service to thank God that one clergyman had felt that the reading of the hymn was the great thing in the service—*while the hymn was being read.*

2. It should never be forgotten that these meetings are meetings for prayer; and hence, undue importance should not be given to speaking, nor

should the remarks be suffered to monopolize the order of exercises. Prayers should be brief, pointed and fervent. The Bible contains over a hundred prayers, and these as having been inspired by the Holy Ghost should be our models. There are only two or three prayers in the Bible that run up to five minutes; of the rest, many of them are so brief as to have been uttered in a single breath. When Peter was sinking amid the angry waves, he did not have time for a general introduction and an eloquent peroration. No! he had barely time to cry out, with intensity of purpose and need, "Lord, save me!" Had he taken more time the waves had swallowed him, and himself had been past all praying. It is said that a minister over a certain charge in the East found one of his prayer-meetings characterized by delay and formalism, and so to remedy this, he took out his watch and said, "Brethren, let us have *sixty* prayers in *sixty* minutes." He got them, and that meeting came to be regarded as one of the most important meetings that that church had ever held.

And thus the element of time becomes very important. The interest and success of the meeting, the number that can take part, and variety in the exercises themselves, will all depend upon the number of minutes that each participant consumes. "In the great noonday prayer-meetings, whose interest and influence are unsurpassed, this is reckoned so important, that none are allowed to occupy more than three or five minutes. What is said should come from the heart in earnest, telling words. Lengthy exhortations are not effective, except in special cases. A leaf from the day's or week's experience, new light that has been shed upon some passage of God's Word, the expression of a burden or a request—some of these things that lie nearest and freshest in our hearts, we may be sure will add much to the interest and success of the prayer-meeting; but beyond that, we need to have the way pointed out very clearly if we go. If we make a mistake in regard to the time, let it be on the side of brevity."

At the opening of the meeting it would be very appropriate to have a few brief prayers, with especial supplications for the increased manifestations of the Spirit's presence and power. "Nothing can make up for His absence. But if He be there (and no one is more ready to come) there is no estimating the good every church may do in its weekly prayer-meetings, do they but act up to their duty and their privilege."

We have already indicated in Chapter III. how subjects of special prayer may be discovered for each meeting. As you visit your people, carry the interest of the prayer-meeting with you, and be alert to discover the spiritual wants of your people that are just then most urgent; and formulate these into appropriate requests for prayer, and either before or at the time of the meeting, and in connection with any written requests for prayer that may have been handed in, ask some one to pray for each particular case; to the end that precious and useful lives may be spared, that the erring may be restored, that the tempted may be victorious, that the youth of the church may be led to Christ, that unconverted ones may find their Saviour, that "weak hands and feeble knees" may be confirmed, and that grace and strength may be imparted to each and to all for the systematic growth in grace of the whole church, and to the glory of God. "Pray for one another."

3. *Remarks.* Let us suppose that you have arranged a plan for the next meeting. You have given out the subject, or it is already known from the printed list, and you want several speakers. Very well: go and ask those you want, and secure their promise to be on hand and take the part assigned them. And that there may be considerable variety in the exercises, would it not be well to select two or three elderly persons, two or three middle-aged, and

two or three young men, if you require that number of speakers for each meeting? In this way all classes will be represented, and due prominence given to each. And especially ought converts to be encouraged to openly confess and acknowledge Christ. It is a critical period with them; if they now come in to be silent members, the longer they continue silent, the more difficult it will be for them to speak and pray in public. At this time, it is comparatively easy for them to take part, for their experience is new and their hearts are full.

4. Singing. This is an important part of the exercises in the successive meetings. Spiritual singing will prove half of the whole meeting in the way of interest, profit, and success. The hymns should have point and life, and such organic connection with the progressive movement of the meeting, that they shall fit into their place, and be "the genuine outgrowth of the state of feeling at that particular point in the meeting." Hence the hymns cannot, except in a general way, be selected in advance of the meeting. A meeting may be made to drag, and prove tedious by the singing of long hymns, lengthened by a chorus to each verse. Some have found it to be an excellent rule not to sing more than two or three verses at a time. "Let us think," says Dr. W. M.

Taylor, "of what the sacrifice of praise is designed to do.' It prepares the way for the descent of the Holy Spirit into the heart. Bring me a minstrel, said Elisha, and while listening to the music, the Spirit of the Lord came down, and he prophesied. Very frequently, through the music of the song of praise, the Spirit of God in His glory has come down and filled the living temple of the human heart. I heard the beautiful story about Toplady's conversion. He went into a barn in Ireland, where he heard a primitive Methodist minister preach the Gospel. At the close, the minister gave out the hymn, 'Come ye sinners, poor and wretched.' It seemed to him then that the whole company took up the appeal from the minister's lips, and instead of one appeal there was that of hundreds. Then he gave his heart to Christ, and nobly did he honor the obligation in his later life, by laying on the altar of Christ the hymn that we are so fond of—

'Rock of Ages, cleft for me,
 Let me hide myself in Thee.'

Then again, singing sustains the heart in trial. Very often in this country we are in the habit of serenading our great men, but oh! no songs in the ear of God are like the sounds which go up from the hearts of God's children in the night of trial. He comes forth from His throne to speak words of comfort and cheer. Then again, it braces the heart for conflict. After his last supper, Christ sang an hymn—the Lord Jesus sang, and sang with Gethsemane in view, to brace himself up for conflict with the prince of this world. Who does not know, too, how Luther strung himself up for his Reformation work by that noble version of the forty-sixth Psalm, termed the Marseillaise of the Reformation." "Let the word of Christ dwell in you richly in all wisdom; teaching and admonishing one another in psalms, and hymns, and spiritual songs, singing with grace in your hearts to the Lord."—Col. 3: 16.

5. Voluntary parts. It will be wise to have a place in every meeting for voluntary remarks. It should be our object to so conduct the meetings that eventually all its parts shall become voluntary; but in the meantime, so long as we cannot realize that in practice, there should be opportunity for every one to use the privilege. There may be strangers present, and these should be invited to take part; or some one may feel that he has something especial to say, and such should have the seasonable opportunity in which to say it. With the utmost liberty of this kind, no reasonable objection can be urged against

THE PRAYER-MEETING. 103

the selection of a plan, which aims to obtain continuous movement in the parts of the meeting, and unity and progress in all the exercises. "Let everything be done decently and in order."

6. Length of meetings. Uniform experience has limited the meeting to an "hour of prayer." Open and dismiss promptly. Do not wait for the people to come. Open promptly, even if you are the only one there, and if no one else should come, why, as Spurgeon says, "have it all to yourself; and if you are asked how many were present, you can say, 'Four.' 'Four! how so?' 'Why, there was myself, and God the Father, God the Son, and God the Holy Ghost; and we had a rich and a real communion together." And also be as prompt in dismissing as in opening; so that the people may know just what to expect, and how to govern their engagements of friendship and business. If there is to be any variation, let it be in favor of a shorter rather than a longer session. Send the people away unwearied and they will come again.

Is it not evident, that such animated interest as judicious planning, working and praying—the united effort of pastor and people—would create in behalf of the prayer-meeting, would at once place and keep the church on a revival basis?

CHAPTER XII.

Variety in Successive Meetings.

Perhaps one reason why prayer-meetings are not more largely attended and enjoyed is found in their stereotype character. When you have attended one prayer-meeting of the church, you can tell what the rest will be like; for you have only to multiply by fifty-two in order to get the result for a whole year. In such cases it might be well to relieve the monotony and introduce greater variety by means of a change in the successive meetings. And with this end in view it might not be inexpedient to leave the people in doubt about the precise nature of the next meeting as to its plan, that thus they may come to it in a state of expectation. Variety in this respect might do much to sustain an interest in the meetings from week to week, and make them more generally attractive. Happy is he who both excites an interest and rewards it.

The continued interest in the temperance reform, which, like a tidal wave, is sweeping over the land, is due, first to the subject, and next to the method the leaders have adopted of introducing new speakers at each meeting, and having as a rule short speeches from each. Although it is the same subject, yet the new speakers that are constantly coming forward give novelty and freshness to the theme by their varied experiences while under the power of drink and its terrible temptations; and in their confessions and aspirations for a better life, they call for sympathy and help. Truth is stranger than fiction, and nothing is more interesting than life in its struggles, defeats and victories. We might learn a valuable lesson from their methods for the conduct of our prayer-meetings.

Let us then enumerate some methods of variety for the conduct of successive meetings, that from these such selection may be made as circumstances require and the topics themselves will permit.

1. Conduct the meeting in the usual way, and make as much as possible out of a method endeared by practice, and rendered valuable by the associations of the past.

2. Let the next meeting be conducted as a Bible Reading on some absorbing theme of life and doctrine. It will be necessary for the leader to carefully collect and classify all the passages of Scripture bearing upon the chosen subject and then assign the texts

to the members, that they may be read in the order in which they have been numbered. The leader must secure a rapid movement for the readings and connect them by such remarks and anecdotes as will illustrate their application and teaching. At proper places prayer and song may be introduced, that thus the whole may be joined together and have unity and power.

3. Variety may still further be secured by the announcement that the next meeting will be conducted on the voluntary plan. The topic should be announced, however, as nothing would be gained by leaving this an open issue. It may be stated, then, that on next week everything from first to last shall be voluntary, as " the Spirit may give utterance " and direction; and in connection with this, all should be urged to come with the desire and the expectation of taking part. Urge some to come with passages of Scripture, or verses from devotional hymns, to read or recite at a moment when there is danger of a " long pause," and in this way the meeting will prove as profitable and interesting as any that might be more carefully arranged for.

4. After the voluntary plan has been tried, it might be well to go to the other extreme and arrange for everything so far as designating the speakers and those who are to pray are concerned.

The remarks should be directed to the topic, and those asked to pray should be requested to pray with special reference to the spiritual wants of the church, for the pastor, for the Sunday school, for the prayer-meeting, for the sick, for the afflicted, for the tried and tempted, and such other and kindred themes as the changing and growing needs of a community would be continually suggesting. Of course, it is understood that the remarks and prayers are to be extempore and under the guidance of the Holy Spirit. In all our proceedings we should seek the presence of Christ, the love of God, and the teaching and illuminating power of the Holy Spirit.

> "I need Thee every hour:
> Teach me Thy will;
> And Thy rich promises
> In me fulfill."

The prayer-meeting is not a debating society, but a meeting of the household of Christ, gathered for mutual sympathy, reciprocal Christian love, and the formation of a noble character.

5. In some churches it might not be amiss to conduct a meeting occasionally in which the reading of essays and correspondence shall take the place of set remarks and exhortations. The best time for such an order, would be the evening set apart to the "Monthly Concert," when a missionary topic is under consideration. It would not be difficult, perhaps, to secure

correspondence from missionaries in foreign and home fields, letters from members that are traveling at home or abroad, and from former pastors and members who have gone to other churches; these would doubtless be glad to send their greetings and stir up the pure minds of the brethren to greater zeal and activity, and such a method as this is entirely Scriptural; for Paul concludes his first letter to the "Thessalonians" in these words:—"I charge you by the Lord that this epistle be read unto all the holy brethren." See also Col. 4: 16.

And in addition to one or two letters that might be secured in this way, members of the church—and the lady members more particularly—might be asked to prepare papers on the particular topic, to set forth the extent of the work in the particular field under view, the manners and customs of the people, their social religious and political life, helps and hindrances to the spread of the Gospel among them, their present urgent need, and other related themes. The preparation for a meeting of this kind would tend to promote the reading of history, develop a valuable literary taste and lay the foundation for intellectual culture.

6. A change of leaders has been tried in some churches with good results. Such method will develop the lay talent in a church, make them feel that the prayer-meeting is their meeting, and that they are

responsible for its success, as well as create a confidence in their ability to conduct a good meeting. It will prevent the prayer-meeting from collapsing in case the church is without a pastor, or in case the pastor is absent on duties connected with his denomination, or the church at large. It will also serve to run the prayer-meeting successfully through the pastor's vacation; for unless the interest is kept up continuously, the church too will take a vacation, and when the pastor returns he will discover that his church has not been growing in grace, but the rather losing ground under the inroads of a worldly spirit.

7. Lastly, such special services as New Year's, Praise, Promise and Memorial-meetings may be provided for in their appropriate season.

But whatever be the method, whether the same plan is continuously followed or such variety is introduced as this chapter contemplates, there is no plan in itself that will guarantee success. That will depend upon spiritual conditions, and the time, prayer, study and effort which the leader shall give to the execution of the plan, and such enthusiasm for his plans as he may be able to awaken in his people. "Study to show thyself approved unto God, a workman that needeth not to be ashamed, rightly dividing the word of truth."

CHAPTER XIII.

THE IMPORTANCE OF THE PRAYER-MEETING.

It is as important for the church in its collective capacity, to sustain the prayer-meeting, as it is for the individual believer to keep up his secret devotions. The Christian cannot grow in grace and in the knowledge of our Lord and Saviour Jesus Christ; in spirituality and in power, without daily communion with God in prayer. This is the experience of both laymen and preachers. "Whenever a Christian backslides," says Spurgeon, "his wandering commences in his closet. I speak what I have felt. I have often gone back from God—never so as to fall finally, I know, but I have often lost that savor of His love which I once enjoyed. I have had to cry,

> 'Those peaceful hours I once enjoyed,
>   How sweet their memory still!
> But they have left an aching void,
>   The world can never fill.'

"I have gone up to God's house to preach, without either fire or energy; I have read the Bible and there has been no light upon it; I have tried to have communion with God, but all has been a failure.

Shall I tell where that commenced? It commenced in my closet. I had ceased in a measure to pray. Here I stand and do confess my faults; I do acknowledge that whenever I depart from God it is there it doth begin. O, Christians, would you be happy? Be much in prayer. Would you be victorious? Be much in prayer.

> 'Restraining prayer, we cease to fight,
> Prayer makes the Christian's armor bright.'

"Mrs. Berry used to say, 'I would not be hired out of my closet for a thousand worlds.' Mr. Jay said, 'If the twelve apostles were living near you, and you had access to them, if this intercourse drew you from the closet, they would prove a real injury to your souls.' Prayer is the ship which bringeth home the richest freight. It is the soil which yields the most abundant harvest."

Nor can churches enjoy any great measure of success in saving souls, unless they are praying churches. Praying churches will be revival churches —such will grow and prosper spiritually and temporally. Would you have a successful church; go and get them to pray; go and get them to cultivate the "power of the knees," not only in their closets, but in their prayer-meetings. "Sirs," says Spurgeon, "I have no opinion of the churches of the present day that do not pray. I go from chapel to chapel in this metropolis, and I see pretty good congregations: but I go to their prayer-meetings on a week evening, and I see a dozen persons. Can God bless us, can He pour out His Spirit upon us, while such things as these exist? He could, but it would not be according to the order of His dispensations, for he says, 'When Zion travails she brings forth children.' Go to your churches and chapels with this thought, that you want more prayer. Go home and say to your minister, 'Sir, we must have more prayer.' We must have an outpouring of real devotion, or else what is to become of many of our churches? O! may God awaken us all, and stir us up to pray, for when we pray we shall be victorious. I should like to take you this morning as Samson did the foxes, tie the firebrands of prayer to you, and send you in among the shocks of corn till you burn the whole up. I should like to make a conflagration by my words, and set all the churches on fire, till the whole has smoked like a sacrifice up to God's throne."

And the reason for this is evident. The Spirit is present with the believer as an unseen presence; "for he dwelleth with you and shall be in you." The Spirit is given by measure to the believer according to the extent that the manifestation of His presence and power has been sought in prayer. To the Son God gave not His Spirit by measure, but the Spirit abode with him in His infinite fulness. With men, however, He dwells to the extent of their earnest seeking and finite capacity. As the Holy Spirit is already with the believer, His presence with an assembly or a prayer-meeting must mean that each one receives a larger portion of the Spirit, so that His presence is with power and demonstration. Beneath this divine outpoural all hearts melt, and they feel, with Jacob of old, "How dreadful is this place! this is none other but the house of God, and this the gate of heaven." It was after the apostles had continued with one accord in prayer and supplication, that the day of Pentecost came with open manifestations of the Spirit's presence and power. The Spirit is poured out upon the assembly either visibly as at Penetcost (Acts 2: 33), or manifestly and feelingly as at a subsequent time, when "the disciples had prayed, the place was shaken where they were, and they were *all filled* with the Holy Ghost, and they spake the word of God with boldness" (Acts 4: 31).

We have all doubtless attended meetings where we felt the Spirit to be present with power and demonstration, that is, when He was poured out upon the assembly in their collective capacity, and in answer to prayer, (Luke 11: 9-13), was present to convict, convert and regenerate. In the revival mceetings held here last year, Major Whittle related an incident to illustrate this, which he had gathered from reliable sources in Kentucky. He was told that Tom Marshall when a student at college was present at a revival meeting, but at a certain stage got up and hastily left the room; for he felt, as he afterwards confessed, that he could not much longer have held out against the influence of the meeting. He was unwilling to give his heart to Christ, for he seemed convinced if he became a Christian, it would become his duty to relinquish his cherished profession, and become a preacher of the Gospel. Now where the church, through lack of prayer and consecration, is cold or lukewarm, or formal and indifferent, one is not oppressed and burdened with such convictions of duty, the Holy Spirit is not poured out upon them, and there is no increased manifestation of His presence and power. Piety will rise no higher in the church than it rises in the prayer-meeting. "I would not unite with a certain church," said a certain man, "because I know its members."

Nor can the importance of the prayer-meeting to the church and the community at large be over-estimated. Heat up the prayer-meeting and the fires of secret devotion will burn more brightly. Heat up the prayer-meeting and you will heat up the pulpit.

Ministers will preach with power when they have a praying church. "O!" said Spurgeon, "had you seen an apostolic church, what a different thing it would appear to one of our churches! as different, I had almost said, as light from darkness; as different as the shallow brook that is dried by summer is from the mighty rolling river, ever full, ever deep and clear, and ever rushing into the sea. Now, where is our prayerfulness compared with theirs; I trust that we know something of the power of prayer here, but I do not think we pray as they did! They broke bread from house to house, and did eat their meat with singleness of heart, giving glory to God. There was not a member of the church, as a rule, who was half-hearted; they gave their souls wholly to God; and, when Ananias and Sapphira divided the price, they were smitten with death for their sin. O! if we prayed as deeply and as earnestly as they did, we should have as much success. Any measure of success we may have had here has been entirely owing, under God, to your prayers; and wherever I have gone, I have boasted that I have a praying people. Let other ministers have as prayerful a people; let missionaries have as many prayers from the Church; and, all things being equal, God will bless them, and there will be greater prosperity than ever."

CHAPTER XIV.

How to Make Prayer-Meetings Interesting.

Not the least of the services which Mr. Moody and his co-laborers have rendered to the evangelism of to-day is the attention they have called to the conduct of the prayer-meeting, and how to make them interesting. Mr. Moody is well qualified to speak on this subject, inasmuch as his experience now covers nearly twenty years of service, in connection with the great noonday prayer-meetings of Chicago and his own church there, as well as, since leaving Chicago, with Christian workers in England and America. His views should be attentively considered. This chapter, then, is a transcript of his talks on the prayer-meeting, in answer to questions put to him in the "Ministerial Conventions," which were held in New York City in 1876, and in Boston in 1877.

I. THE NEW YORK CONVENTION.

I think this is one of the most important questions which can come before us. I believe more ministers fail right here than in any

THE PRAYER-MEETING. 117

other place. Where one fails in a pulpit, I believe fifty fail in the prayer-meeting. I have noticed as I have been traveling up and down the country, and mingling with a great many ministers, that it is not the man that preaches the best that is most successful. You must get the people to pray.

It is so much easier to preach to an audience who are praying for you than to those who are criticising you all the while. Now I find it a great help in a prayer-meeting to get the people close together ; if they won't come, I would take the chair and walk down amongst them. Then another important thing is to see that the ventilation is all right. A good many meetings are held in basements and small rooms, where there is no ventilation, where the windows, perhaps, won't be opened through the winter ; where people get sleepy, and you think it is your fault. See that it is not too hot or too cold, and that the air is pure. It is a good thing to have a subject, suppose "faith," or "love," and let people know it a week before. Let the minister not always lead, for then when he goes off there is a collapse. If he manages right, it seems to me, he would get different leaders, so that when he goes off there will be no falling away. You may ask what we are going to do with those men who talk so long. Well, I would see them privately, and say, "Now, try to be a little shorter." It would be a good thing, however, if the ministers would show a good example. They very often leave just fifteen minutes for the meeting, and complain of Deacon Jones taking up the rest of the time. They say everything they can think of on the chapter, and wonder why "the poor laymen won't take it up." Why, if they say everything they can think of on a certain chapter, there is not much chance for a poor layman, especially if he don't know what the chapter is to be. If a man takes part in a meeting, he has got a little more interest in it. There is a good deal of truth in what the old deacon said, that he always liked the meeting when he took part, and he didn't care for it when he didn't take part.

A delegate observed that the Congregational churches in New England had a rule that the minister should lead the prayer-meetings, for this reason: that it was found when ministers took the place of laymen in this matter, the latter took the leadership out of his hands. He asked Mr. Moody what he would do to prevent that. Mr. Moody replied that this was not his experience on the subject. Dr. Kirk, of Boston, of whose church he was a member twenty years ago, very seldom led the meeting; neither did Dr. Cuyler usually lead in his own church prayer-meeting in Brooklyn.

Q. Ought the minister to call on people to pray and speak? A. My theory is one and my practice another. I have always advocated open prayer-meetings, but very often people get up whom we know nothing about, and talk too long, so I have lately to put the meeting in the hands of those on the platform.

Q. Is it right to call on a man to pray when he is not in the spirit of prayer? A. He should be in the spirit of prayer: but that is one of the things which makes me object to call on men to pray.

Q. What would you do with a brother who prays the same prayer over and over? A. I should see him privately and talk to him about his own soul.

Q. Suppose you drive him away? A. Let him go. Five will come and take his place.

Q. Is it wise to adhere to a series of topics? A. If it is in the way throw it overboard; don't have a cast-iron rule.

Q. Would it be well to make the Sunday-school lesson the subject for the prayer-meeting? A. If you have teachers' meetings better not. If you have not teachers' meetings I have known it to work pretty well.

Q. Shall the women take part in our church prayer-meetings? A. It is a controverted point. Let every prayer-meeting have its own way.

Q. What about ringing the bell when a man is praying? A. If the prayer don't go any further than his own head I would have no scruple in ringing the bell.

II. THE BOSTON CONVENTION.

Q. What shall we do with the awful pauses in our meetings? A. They can be avoided, I think, if the minister is free and social and makes every one feel at home. These pauses are just the times when that man or that lady who is not in the habit of speaking, can read a verse from God's Word which they have found precious to their souls. In this way they can gain confidence to speak. A good many people have an idea that they must follow the minister and preach a sort of sermon; but a word from the Bible often carries great comfort.

Q. Would you have children in the large prayer-meetings? A. Well, there is danger in that. One great danger which is likely to beset children is spiritual pride. A great many people in the church, unfortunately, are foolish enough if a little boy speaks for Christ in a touching way to praise him; and that makes him very proud. I should not like to have my child praised in this way. Children learn the sweetness of praise soon enough in the world. I should be a little afraid of having boys and girls encouraged to jump up in the large prayer-meetings.

Q. Do you favor boys' prayer-meetings? A. By all means, I have found no meetings more blessed in the work of conversion. The boys and the girls should meet by themselves under the direction of some older person of experience as a leader. I have been very much interested in the meetings for little boys conducted here by Mr. Hastings.

Q. How shall we get women to speak in prayer-meetings? A. Well, if the meeting is free and social, as I said, I don't think there will be any who are afraid to speak. There are two ways of conducting a prayer-meeting. The minister may enter the room with his coat buttoned up, and looking neither to the right nor the left, take the desk and either go through the reading of a long hymn or make a long prayer. Of course a meeting begun in this way is stiff and formal, and there will be no sense of freedom. Then there is another way. The minister may enter the room in a friendly and social way, shaking hands with everybody and saying a pleasant word to all, and perhaps he will get the friends to select the opening hymn or ask some lady to read a passage of Scripture, and the meeting will be begun before they know it. If everybody would carry the Scriptures to the meetings there would be no trouble in keeping the meetings interesting.

Q. Would you announce a subject for prayer previous to the meeting? A. I would. It has been done in our church in Chicago, and it has been a great help to our prayer-meetings. We want to have these meetings a sort of family gathering where a mother who has a son out of Christ can bring him before Jesus, and the whole church bear up her petition to the Lord. United prayer in faith that God will answer our petitions will surely bring back the blessing.

Q. Would you encourage women to speak? A. In a social prayer-meeting I would encourage any one to speak. We want to get all Christians at work in the service of Christ.

Q. Do you believe in having different ones to lead the meeting? A. Well, that plan has been tried. Dr. Cuyler found it very successful in his church in Brooklyn. He often takes a seat among the congregation while the leader conducts the prayer-meeting. One great secret of success is to get others to work. I would rather get ten men to work than do ten men's work myself.

Q. How ought prayer-meetings to be conducted in a church without a pastor? A. With as much earnestness as possible. Sometimes God blesses specially a church when it is without a pastor because they trust in His grace and not in any arm of flesh.

Q. How would you break up the habit of long prayers? A. I think ministers need find no trouble, if they are honest with their people. They like real plain talk. I should speak to a man making long prayers privately, not publicly, and say to him: "Your prayers need a little more unction, they are too long for the meeting." Exhortation ought not to take the place of prayer, but it is better to have an exhortation than a prayerless prayer. That is an abomination in the sight of God and men. Some people seem to keep on praying because they don't know where to stop. Let there be always a distinct object in prayer. I have been dissatisfied at some of the men's prayer-meetings in the Tabernacle because men prayed for nothing but merely exhorted. The other night a man was telling God how great he was and how wonderfully he had made man; and a godly old saint who was better acquainted with the Lord said, "Just ask him for something."

Q. Suppose a man won't heed your advice to make prayer short? A. I should speak to him again and again, and if that did not bring about the result, I would rebuke him publicly. I would have a bell at the meeting. One word—don't rely on your prayers, but on Christ. Always remember that the salvation of Jesus is free, and that all may have it by simply taking it.

Q. When do you consider a prayer to be too long? A. Well, if the prayer-meeting is about an hour long, which I think about the proper length, it certainly can't be right for two or three men to take up the time. If a man has the cause of the Jews on his heart let him pray for them and then stop. It is awful to open one's eyes and see that a man is teaching his own views or criticising the opinions of other people when he seems to be praying. It chills me right through.

Q. What would you do if a man, whose piety the church distrusts, attempts to speak? A. I would never allow him to speak. The best way is to deal fairly and squarely with people. I would rather hurt a man's feelings than to have the Church injured. A man who pays fifty cents on the dollar when he could pay one hundred cents on the dollar had better keep still.

CHAPTER XV.

Uniform Topics.

If there is any advantage in having a list of topics for an entire year, would not uniformity in all the churches secure the same benefits on an enlarged scale? That system in our public schools which takes the scholar from the "Kindergarten" progressively along until he graduates in the "High School," is wise and economical. The main fault to be found with the American scheme of education is this that it does not extend far enough. It would be an advantage to have an international system by which all our schools should have a common basis and run parallel with each other by successive steps from the "Kindergarten" to the University; and have such organic connection that a student would require no change in text-books and lose no rank in removing from Peoria to Chicago, or from New York to Boston. The Prussian system of education is doubtless more comprehensive than our own in this respect, and it is well known that German scholarship is thorough-going and profound. The greater efficiency of a people, generally and systematically educated, over one less so, was well illustrated in the conduct and the speedy termination of the late French-Prussian war. A gun is all the more effective for being held and controlled by a well-trained mind. The rank and file of the Prussian army were highly educated, and prince and peasant stood side by side for the patriotic defense of their fatherland.

The writer expressed his views on this subject in an article that was published in the *Interior* a year ago, which are reproduced at this place, and were as follows: The fact that uniform subjects for Sunday-school study have been adopted in nearly all the Bible lands of the world shows the value that has been set upon system. Let us suppose that the Bible is so divided into chapters for daily reading, and verses for the thorough and systematic study of all the facts of the Bible, that the scholar is taken through the entire Bible once in seven years. Who does not see the advantage of such method in study? The feeling that all Christians the world over, on a given Sabbath are reading and studying the same portion of Scripture, is very stimulating and significant. And besides, since the time this method has been adopted there has been a growing interest given to Bible study. It has stimulated explorations and geographical surveys in Palestine; and the commentaries, lesson-leaves, maps and helps of one kind and another called into circulation by it, can scarcely be over-estimated for value and importance.

Now, then, would not something similar be beneficial for the prayer-meeting? If the former plan for study gives us the facts and principles of religion, why might not a series of topics be selected for each year that shall be especially adapted to the needs of daily Christian life, to Christian nurture and doctrine? In many of our churches the Sunday-school lesson has been used as the topic for the prayer-meeting. That plan has some advantages; for instruction on systematic topics is far preferable to subjects selected at random. But a little different class of topics would prove more suitable for the prayer-meeting, namely the arrangement of Biblical truth with reference to daily life and growth in grace. Edification implies system, order and progress. By this plan, praise and promise meetings and special occasions might be suitably provided for, and all classes of Christians systematically edified. (Eph. 4:12-16.) This would secure unity in the services of the prayer-meeting and give opportunity for all to come with special prayer and preparation with reference to a set topic.

It may be objected that by a plan like this the special needs of a particular congregation at a particular time might be overlooked and neglected. That is true, but the remedy is simple. At such a time omit the topic, make your own selection, annex appropriate texts of Scripture, and give notice in due time that the change has been made. But in the long run, nothing will be gained by making religion spasmodic. Nothing will more establish Christian life, faith and doctrine, than faithful induction into all the great Christian truths that edify the body of Christ. Is not the Bible Reading and the Bible Study which form so prominent a feature of the great revival of our day; nay, is not, in part, the revival itself under the Divine blessing, a result of the increased piety—prayer and work—which the uniform lessons have been instrumental in promoting in the ranks of the laity? Would not the adoption of uniformity in suitable topics for the prayer-meeting further the same end and make Christian life more and more like the shining light in Prov. 4:18?

And in this connection the writer will add an extract from an article "On Uniform Topics for The Prayer-Meeting," which was furnished the *Interior* by the facile pen of the Rev. John Locke Martin, and is as follows: "The heading and its embodied idea are not original with me, but I would like to add my mite of a word to help along this idea to a practical end. I have seen no suggestion of late which seems so promising of real benefit in our church work as this one of a uniform series of topics for the prayer-meeting. The very presentation of the subject should be sufficient to lead to its hearty adoption, for it has every thing in its favor. I know not whether the experience is general, but find it to be the case with all with whom I have conversed, that one of the great hindrances toward making the prayer-meeting a success is a want of unity in the services, and therefore a want of special prayer and preparation on the part of the members. To simply announce from the pulpit on Sabbath the subject for the next week-day is not enough. Very frequently some of the best attendants at the prayer-meeting are absent from the sanctuary services, and so miss the announcement. But if, like the Sabbath-school lesson, there was a printed series of topics, this, out of many objections would be avoided,—every one could know the topic. It is beyond question that the uniform system of Sabbath-school lessons has been a great help and blessing in this work. By this means we have reaped the benefit of system, which is the key-note of all successful work, and have stimulated a degree of Bible study never known before. And all of these advantages would accrue to the prayer-meeting if such a system would only be adopted by the different churches. It is simply a waste of writing to say that our prayer-meetings need all the helpful means that can be secured; for have not their dullness and coldness become proverbial?"

And the following list of topics is another commentary upon the article in whose favor Mr. Martin wrote with such choice terms of approbation. And here just a word of explanation may be proper. The writer was invited by the Rev. M. B. Lowrie to unite with him "in getting up a list of subjects for the coming year for our two churches." This was accepted with the understanding that other churches should be asked to join with us. A list was then prepared by consultation, and in its present form is mainly due to the selection of the Revs. M. B. Lowrie and J. M. Waddle. A copy of it was also published in the *Interior*, and other churches, if they saw their way clear, were cordially invited to unite with us in its use. So far as known to the writer this list is now being used with profit and acceptance by the following churches: Galesburg, Rev. M. B. Lowrie, pastor; Kirkwood, Rev. E. W. Thompson;

Knoxville, Rev. J. M. Waddle; Lewistown, Rev. J. F. Magill; Mt. Sterling, Rev. J. G. Lowrie; Onarga, Rev. W. D. Magner; Peoria Calvary Mission, Rev. John Weston; Peoria Grace, Rev. H. S. Beavis; and Peoria Second, Rev. Lewis O. Thompson.

TOPICS.

Jan. 2. Opening of the year. Ex. 13: 10; Deut. 14: 22; Ps. 102; 24-28; Deut. 32: 7.

" 9. The Sympathy of Jesus. John 11.

" 16. Working for God every day. Ps. 96: 2; Heb. 3: 13; Matth. 21: 28.

" 23. The Work of the Holy Spirit. Zech. 12: 10; Jno. 16: 8-14; Ro. 8: 16.

" 30. Prayer for Schools. Is. 54: 13; Dan. 1: 17; Prov. 1: 5; Hos. 4: 6.

Feb. 6. Monthly Concert. China and the Chinese in America. Ps. 2: 8.

" 13. The Helping Hand. Gal. 6: 1-10.

" 20. Sources of Christian Life and Growth. Acts 20: 32; John 15: 4; Deut. 8: 3; 1 Pet. 2: 2.

" 27. Out into the Highways. Luke 14: 16-24; Mark 10: 46.

Mar. 6. Monthly Concert. Mexico and N. Mex. Ps. 119: 130.

" 13. Why Read the Bible? Jno. 20: 31; 2 Tim. 3: 15-17; 1 Thes. 2: 13; 1 Ki. 2: 3.

" 20. How to Read the Bible. Acts 17: 11; Job 23: 12; Jer. 15: 16.

" 27. Work and Wages. Matth. 20: 1-16.

April 3. Control of the Tongue. Jas. 1: 26; Jas. 3: 5-13; Matth. 12: 36; Ps. 141: 3.

" 10. Monthly Concert. India. Dan. 7: 14.

" 17. Seed Time. Ec. 11: 6; Ps. 126: 6.

" 24. Psalm 34.

THE PRAYER-MEETING. 129

May   1. Temperance. Eph. 5:18; Ps. 94:20.
"   8. Monthly Concert. Siam and Laos. Ro. 10:14-15.
"   15. The Believer's Relation to Christ. John 15:1-8; Ro. 8:17; Eph. 5:30.
"   22. Personal Religion. Ps. 27:8; Ps. 17:4-9; 1 Cor. 9:27; Ps. 39:1.
"   29. Family Religion. 2 Samuel 6:20; Gen. 18:19; Josh. 24:15.
June 5. Monthly Concert. Africa. Ps. 68:31.
"   12. Christ's Love for his Church. Jno. 10:11; Eph. 5:25-26; Eph. 4:11-13.
"   19. Gospel Manna. Ex. 16:15; Jno. 6:48; Ps. 119:103.
"   26. Under the Juniper Tree. 1 Kings 19:4; Jer. 20:7-9; Ps. 73.
July 3. Christian Patriotism. 1. Sam. 12:20-25; Deut. 17:18-20; Ro. 10:1
"   10. Monthly Concert. N. American Indians. 1 Cor. 9:16-17.
"   17. How to keep the Sabbath. Ex. 20:8-11; Luke 14:1-25; Neh. 13:15-23.
"   24. My Duty to the Prayer-Meeting. Heb. 10:25; Mal. 3:16.
"   31. The Promises attending the Word. Is. 55:10; 1 Pet. 1:18-25.
Aug. 7. Psalm 27.
"   14. Monthly Concert. South America. Prov. 14:34.
"   21. Planning for Business. Jas. 4:13; Luke 12:18; Deut. 31:12-13.
"   28. The Trials of Faith. Gen. 22:1; Matth. 15:21; id. 16:21; Mark 7:24; id. 8:26.
Sept. 4. Monthly Concert. Japan. John 4:9-10.
"   11. Advantages of Christian Society. Acts 28:15; 1 Thes. 3:1; Jno. 11:5.
"   18. Confession of Sin. Hos. 5:15; Ps. 51:3.
"   25. Helps and Hindrances to Spiritual Prosperity. Prov. 30:7-9; Luke 12:13-21.

Oct.	2.	The Earth bringeth forth Fruit. Ps. 65 : 11. Mark 4 : 28 ; Deut. 33 : 14 ; Heb. 3 : 17.
"	9.	Monthly Concert. Persia. Matth. 2 : 12.
"	16.	The Danger of neglecting the Gospel. Heb. 2 : 3.
"	23.	The Connection of Peace with Faith. Ro. 5 : 1.
"	30.	Christ's Death for Sin. Is. 53 ; Ro. 5 : 8.
Nov.	6.	Monthly Concert. Papal Europe. Ro. 1 : 15.
"	13.	The Bible Doctrine of Conscience. Jer. 6 : 15 ; 1 Tim. 4 : 2 ; Heb. 9 : 14 ; Acts. 23 : 1.
"	20.	Visiting the Sick and Helping the Destitute. Jas. 1 : 27 ; Matth. 25 : 40.
"	27.	Reasons for Thankfulness. Eph. 5 : 20.
Dec.	4.	Monthly Concert. Syria. Acts 13 : 44-49.
"	11.	Honor God with thy Substance. Prov. 3 : 9.
"	18.	Patience under Discouragements. Rev. 2 : 3-7 ; Acts 27 : 33.
"	25.	Faithful unto Death. Rev. 2 : 10.

CHAPTER XVI.

Steps Towards Uniformity.

Let us enumerate some of the steps which have been taken by the church at large in the direction of uniform topics for the prayer-meeting.

It may be supposed that the use of the international series of Sunday-school lessons in all Christian lands, and their general adaptability to the purpose for which they have been selected, has given the hint to the prayer-meeting. If that has proved an advantage, why will not this also? Nor need we look upon the exposition of the topics by the religious press as tending to destroy thought, original research and experience; not at all, but rather as illustrations of topical treatment, which, while it does not take the place of thought, may largely invigorate it, and give it a hopeful, useful and intelligent direction. And with this proof of practical benefit which that pioneer, the International Series, from many years of successful trial has already presented, it will be much easier for uniform topics in the prayer-meeting to step into use and favor; for whatever are the objections to be urged against the latter, they apply with equal force against the former.

But uniformity in topics for the prayer-meeting all over the world has been secured for just one week in the year—the Week of Prayer. This shows, when great results are looked for in connection with prayer that uniform action is desirable. But if this is desirable for one week, why is not for fifty-two weeks? And will any one say that the meetings during the Week of Prayer lack interest and profit?

The fact that some churches are in the habit of using the Sunday-school lessons as subjects for the prayer-meeting is an indication that topics with which the people may make themselves familiar are relished better than the custom which gives them no topics at all.

It has already come to the knowledge of the writer, that a number of churches in different parts of the land have united in the use of a list of subjects, besides those mentioned at the close of our last chapter. The first list, as given below, was used last year by the seven Presbyterian churches of Detroit, viz: First Presbyterian, Fort Street; Jefferson Avenue, Westminster, Calvary, Union, and Central.

THE PRAYER-MEETING. 133

TOPICS.

Jan.	5.	"This Year Also." Luke 13:6-9.
"	9.	YOUNG PEOPLE'S MEETING. Wisdom's Call. Prov. 1.
"	10.	The Prayer for Pardon. Ps. 51.
"	11.	Renewal of Covenant. Ezra 10:1-14. Neh. 9:38.
"	12.	PREPARATORY LECTURE.
"	19.	MONTHLY CONCERT. The Outlook. The Last Command. Mark 16:15-20.
"	25.	Prayer for Colleges. Consecrated Learning. Acts 7:20-22; Heb. 11:23-27.
"	26.	The Faithful God. Duet. 7:6-13.
Feb.	2.	MONTHLY CONCERT. China and Chinese in U. S.
"	9.	Christ's Hour of Joy. Luke 10:21-24; Matt. 11:25-30.
"	16.	Misplaced Pity. Luke 23:26-28.
"	23.	A Good Conscience. Job 31:19-32.
Mar.	2.	MONTHLY CONCERT. Mexico and New Mexico.
"	9.	PREPARATORY LECTURE.
"	16.	Ignorant Prayer. Mark 10:35-40.
"	23.	The Helper of Our Infirmities. Rom. 8:26, 27.
✝ "	30.	Prayer and Action. Ex. 14:13-16.
Apr.	6.	MONTHLY CONCERT. India.
"	13.	Micah's Religion. Judges 17.
"	20.	Reward of Self-denial. Matt. 19:27-30.
"	27.	Responsibility Declined. Exod. 4:10-16
May	4.	MONTHLY CONCERT. Siam and Laos.
"	11.	PREPARATORY LECTURE.
"	18.	The Filial Spirit. Rom. 8:14-17.
"	25.	Obscure Workers. Jer. 38:7-13; John 1:40-46.
June	1.	MONTHLY CONCERT. Africa.
"	8.	Youthful Lives Contrasted. 2 Kings 21:1-9; 22.
"	15.	Christ's Standard of Righteousness. Matt. 5:20.
"	22.	The Glory of the Word. Ps. 19:7-14.
"	29.	The Household of God. Eph. 2:19-22.

July 6. PREPARATORY LECTURE.
" 13. MONTHLY CONCERT. N. A. Indians.
" 20. Perpetuated Sin. 2 Kings 17:21–23.
" 27. Telling of Christ. John 4:28–39.
Aug. 3. MONTHLY CONCERT. South America.
" 10. The Severity of Christ. Mal. 3:1–6; Matt. 3:10–12.
" 17. The Year of Jubilee. Levit. 25:10–16; Luke 4:16–30.
" 24. Stumbling at the prosperity of the Wicked. Ps. 73.
" 31. The Christian's Portion. 1 Cor. 3:21–23
Sept. 7. PREPARATORY LECTURE.
" 14. MONTHLY CONCERT. Japan.
" 21. The Complete Body. 1 Cor. 12:14–31.
" 28. Daily Gleaning. Ruth 2:19; 2 Cor. 9:6–11.
Oct. 5. MONTHLY CONCERT. Persia.
" 12. Household Religion. Deut. 6.
" 19. The Service of Song. Eph. 5:18–20.
" 26. The Vanity of Worldly Good. Eccl. 2.
Nov. 2. MONTHLY CONCERT. Papal Europe.
" 9. PREPARATORY LECTURE.
" 16. Heard from the Beginning. Dan. 9:20–23.
" 23. The Law of Edification. 1 Cor. 14:26.
" 30. To Every Man His Work. Mark 13:34; Eph. 4:7.
Dec. 7. MONTHLY CONCERT. Syria.
" 14. The Prayer of Moses. Psalm 90.
" 21. Thomas' Doubt and Faith. John 20:24–31.
" 28 Our House from Heaven. 2 Cor. 5:1–5.

To what extent this second list is being used the writer is unable to say; but some of those who have been previously using prepared topics, speak of the practice in the highest terms.*

---

* The Rev. J. C. McClintock commends it in the following words: "For a year past a number of pastors have used the same topics in their prayer-meetings. The result has been so helpful, that they are uniting in the same plan for 1878, and they ask you to join them in what has proved a delightful means of Communion. The Topics have been furnished by several of our

TOPICS.

Jan.	2.	God's Presence with us.	Ex. 32: 12–23.
"	6. 12. }	The Week of Prayer.	
"	16.	The Gracious Invitation.	Is. 55: 1–9.
"	23.	Will You Accept It?	John 12: 42–50.
"	30.	Prayer for Schools.	Prov. 3: 13–26.
Feb.	6.	Go, Preach the Gospel.	Mark 18: 15–20.
"	13.	The Sinner's Danger.	Gen. 19: 12–22.
"	20.	The Refuge.	Col. 1: 13–22.
"	27.	The Sister's Choice.	Luke 10: 38–42.
Mar.	6.	From Darkness to Light.	Acts 26: 16–23.
"	13.	The Lord's Prayer.	Matt. 6: 5–15.
"	20.	Secret and Family Prayer.	Acts. 10: 1–20.
"	27.	The Prayer of Faith.	Matt. 15: 21–28.
Apr.	3.	Zion's Prospects.	Is. 40: 1–11.
"	10.	What Shall I Do With Jesus?	Matt. 27: 19–35.
"	17.	What May I Do for Jesus?	Matt. 25: 31–40.
"	24.	Not Here, but Risen.	Luke 24: 1–12.
May	1.	What Can She Do?	Mark 14: 1–9.
"	8.	The Comforter.	John 14: 15–27.
"	15.	Thy Poor Brother.	Deut. 15: 7–11.
"	22.	Cure for Thought-Taking.	Matt. 6: 25–35.
"	29.	The Solution of Doubt.	John 7: 1–18.
June	5.	Fields White to Harvest.	John 4: 30–32.
"	12.	The Teacher's Preparation.	Ezra 7: 10–
"	19.	The Teacher's Reward.	Luke 10: 16–24.
"	26.	Quality not quantity.	Judges 7: 1–9.

---

experienced pastors, who have aimed to give a due proportion to Devotion, Doctrine, Christian Experience and Daily Life." "I have been astonished to find so many Churches using Topics of nearly the same form. Let us have them in our Presbyterian Church, THE SAME.—*Rev. J. M. Bishop, Lebanon, Ind.* "I am heartily interested in the scheme. We have used the list for 1877, with great profit."—*Rev. E. P. Whallon, Liberty, Ind.* "There is much good to be derived from these topical prayer-meetings. They keep the Church in a chronic state of revival."—*Rev. J. M. Nourse, Athens, Ohio.* "As to the 'communion prayer-meeting topics,' I am deeply interested."—*Rev. T. H. Clelland, Council Bluffs, Ia.* "I have used the prayer-meeting topics during the past year, with great acceptance to my people."—*Rev. Chas. Little, Wabash, Ind.*

July	3.	Declaration of Dependence. Josh. 24: 21–29.
"	10.	The Friend of Sinners. Luke 7: 40–50.
"	17.	A Prosperous Man. Gen. 39: 1–6.
"	24.	Soul Prosperity. 3 John 1: 8–
"	31.	A Peculiar People. 1 Peter 2: 9–17.
Aug.	7.	Open Doors. Rev. 3: 7–13.
"	14.	Eli's Failure. 1 Sam. 2: 27–36.
"	21.	Two Paths. Gen. 13: 8–18.
"	28.	The Saviour. Acts 13: 23–33.
Sept.	4.	The King. Ps. 2: 1–12.
"	11.	The Shepherd. John 10: 1–10.
"	18.	Astray and Asleep. Jonah 1: 1–12.
"	25.	The Stone Rolled Away. Mark 16: 1–16.
Oct.	2.	Christian Giving. 2 Cor. 9: 5–15.
"	9.	Armor and Strength. 1 Sam. 17: 37–50.
"	16.	The Penitent's Prayer. Ps. 51: 1–19.
"	23.	Saved. 1 John 5: 9–21.
"	30.	Joy. 1 Peter 4: 13–19.
Nov.	6.	Our Work. John 1: 35–49.
"	13.	The Spirit's Work. John 16: 1–14.
"	20.	Daniel—Greatly Beloved. Dan. 9: 17–23.
"	27.	The Year's Blessings. Ps. 65: 1–13.
Dec.	4.	Times of Refreshing. Mal. 3: 10–18.
"	11.	Justified Faith. James 2: 14–26.
"	18.	No Continuing City. Heb. 13: 5–15.
"	25.	Good Tidings. Luke 2: 8–19.

But a movement on a still larger scale has already been inaugurated, the one from Chicago as a center, and the other from London, towards uniformity, which in the means of securing it is a great and important discovery. Its existence came to the knowledge of the writer only a few weeks ago, but happily in time to fit into its place here as another in the series. This plan is already solving the difficulties connected with uniformity. And from the sketch to be introduced it is plain that no single person is entitled to the claim of exclusive discovery. It is evidently the prompting of that same Spirit who has access to all Christian hearts. It is generally the way when He desires to inaugurate and carry forward a great movement that He prepares the way for it by working upon the mind of the Church at large. A perusal of the following sketch from the pen of Miss E. Dryer will more and more convince us of this:

BIBLE READING AND PRAYER ALLIANCE.

The object of this Alliance is to promote the united prayerful study of the Holy Scriptures. Pastors of churches, Superintendents and Teachers of Sabbath Schools, and Christians everywhere, are cordially invited to co-operate in this effort, and to make the seven chapters of the week, or subjects taken therefrom, the frequent theme of meetings for Bible study. Any Christian may organize a class of readers, and thus many unsaved persons may be brought to the teaching of the Word of God.

The Committee who recommend this Alliance is composed of representatives chosen by their respective denominations and societies in the city of Chicago to promote this work.

T. W. HARVEY, Pres. Y. M. C. A., Chairman.
Rev. BISHOP C. E. CHENEY, Reformed Episcopal.
Rev. DR. D. B. CHENEY, Baptist.
Rev. Dr. J. MONRO GIBSON, Presbyterian.
Rev. Dr. E. P. GOODWIN, Congregationalist.
Rev. Dr. EDWARD SULLIVAN, Episcopal.
Rev. DR. JOHN Z. TONGERSON, Lutheran.
Rev. DR. W. C. WILLING, Presiding Elder, M. E. C.
Mrs. W. H. GOODRICH, Bible Work, Cor. Sec. and Treas.
Miss E. DRYER, Bible Work, Rec. Sec'y.

THE BIBLE READING AND PRAYER ALLIANCE had its beginning January 1st, 1877, in a small morning prayer-meeting in Chicago. There was then no purpose of extending it beyond the circle of a few Christian friends. But, in God's providence, so rapidly did the united interest spread, that a Scripture calendar was prepared, and very soon the first five thousand had found their way, *with care*, into churches, Sunday-schools, hospitals, boarding-houses, families, not only in the city, but in different parts of the State and in distant States.

The effort received its first marked impulse in a conference of Christian ladies of different denominations, who met weekly for Bible study and prayer; most of whom were engaged in the active Christian work of cottage prayer-meetings and house to house visitation which attended and followed the Moody meetings of that winter.

These Christian workers were bound together, under the name of the "Bible Work Association," by the following

AGREEMENT:

We, the undersigned, purpose

I. To read the Bible together daily, praying the Holy Spirit to guide us into all truth, according to our Lord's promise : John 16:13.

II. To pray daily for each other, that we may grow in grace and a knowledge of our Lord Jesus Christ; 2 Pet. 3:18.

III. To meet together weekly and monthly for prayer and conference and study of the Scriptures, that we may thereby be better prepared to present to the lost, salvation in Jesus Christ, and to lead His church to seek the things that are above, where He sitteth on the right hand of God; Col. 3:1.

IV. By personal conversations, prayer-meetings, Scripture readings, and other Christian efforts, to present Christ as the Saviour of the lost, and to present help to all who are weary and heavy laden. Matt. 11:28.

In a few months, it was evident that the Lord was extending the work beyond the control of any such organization of active membership as was at first contemplated, and yet not a line had appeared in print concerning it.

In June, the Secretary learned through a newspaper item, that in January, 1876, a similar union was formed in London, under the leadership of the Rev. Thomas Richardson, London, which numbered the first year about 18,000 members, and which has extended, through missionaries, to Arabia, China, Persia and India.

It then became more than ever apparent that our Lord was executing a loving purpose of uniting His Church in prayer and Bible study, in a new and great degree; and increased and systematic efforts were made to establish the wide-spread work which had grown from such small beginnings.

The present Committee, representatives of Evangelical denominations and societies in Chicago, convened in October, 1877, and under the new name organized to promote the objects of this alliance. It was thought best to spend six months in the New Testament and six months in the Old Testament; beginning January with Matthew, and reading the first two gospels and the Pauline epistles; and in June to begin Genesis, reading historic parts of the Old Testament during the remainder of the year.

From these Daily Readings the committee have selected fifty-two topics, which, following the practice instituted at the beginning, may be conveniently used in weekly meetings, and which present the advantage of united study and preparation on the part of those who use them.

A similar course has, during the last year, in some parts of our country, been followed with good results, in church prayer-meetings, cottage meetings, and meetings organized for Bible study.

We hope that in Churches, Sabbath Schools and Christian communities, Christians who are interested to forward this Union of Bible study and prayer, will send us their names at once. We shall issue cards of membership to such, and to all others who, for the year, desire them.

To induce others to read the Bible systematically, is one of the *easy* and *most fruitful* sources of Christian effort.

Old and young, sick and well, may find successful work in this line. One feeble Christian, in a community where there is no church, may through faith and prayerful effort, form a society in which the word of God shall grow, until the sower and reapers shall rejoice together in heaven amid the gathered harvest. Deut. 8:3; Acts 6:7; Acts 17:11; Col. 1:5, 6; John 15:3; Matt. 13:3-9.

God has promised *to bless his own word.* Isa. 55:10, 11; Matt. 24:35.

And the following " Calendar " for Daily Scripture Reading has been prepared by the Committee of the Alliance for the year 1878:

CALENDAR.

JAN.	FEB.	MAR.	APR.	MAY.	JUNE.
1 Matt. 1	1 Mark 4	1 Acts 16	1 1 Cor. 3	1 Gal. 4	1 2 Tim. 1
2 " 2	2 " 5	2 " 17	2 " 4	2 " 5	2 " 2
3 " 3	3 " 6	3 " 18	3 " 5	3 " 6	3 " 3
4 " 4	4 " 7	4 " 19	4 " 6	4 Eph. 1	4 " 4
5 " 5	5 " 8	5 " 20	5 " 7	5 " 2	5 Titus 1
6 " 6	6 " 9	6 " 21	6 " 8	6 " 3	6 " 2
7 " 7	7 " 10	7 " 22	7 " 9	7 " 4	7 " 3
8 " 8	8 " 11	8 " 23	8 " 10	8 " 5	8 Phil. 1
9 " 9	9 " 12	9 " 24	9 " 11	9 " 6	9 Heb. 1
10 " 10	10 " 13	10 " 25	10 " 12	10 Phil. 1	10 " 2
11 " 11	11 " 14	11 " 26	11 " 13	11 " 2	11 " 3
12 " 12	12 " 15	12 " 27	12 " 14	12 " 3	12 " 4
13 " 13	13 " 16	13 " 28	13 " 15	13 " 4	13 " 5
14 " 14	14 Acts 1	14 Rom. 1	14 " 16	14 Col. 1	14 " 6
15 " 15	15 " 2	15 " 2	15 2 Cor. 1	15 " 2	15 " 7
16 " 16	16 " 3	16 " 3	16 " 2	16 " 3	16 " 8
17 " 17	17 " 4	17 " 4	17 " 3	17 " 4	17 " 9
18 " 18	18 " 5	18 " 5	18 " 4	18 1 Thss. 1	18 " 10
19 " 19	19 " 6	19 " 6	19 " 5	19 " 2	19 " 11
20 " 20	20 " 7	20 " 7	20 " 6	20 " 3	20 " 12
21 " 21	21 " 8	21 " 8	21 " 7	21 " 4	21 " 13
22 " 22	22 " 9	22 " 9	22 " 8	22 " 5	22 Gen. 1
23 " 23	23 " 10	23 " 10	23 " 9	23 2 Thss 1	23 " 2
24 " 24	24 " 11	24 " 11	24 " 10	24 " 2	24 " 3
25 " 25	25 " 12	25 " 12	25 " 11	25 " 3	25 " 4
26 " 26	26 " 13	26 " 13	26 " 12	26 1 Tim. 1	26 " 5
27 " 27	27 " 14	27 " 14	27 " 13	27 " 2	27 " 6
28 " 28	28 " 15	28 " 15	28 Gal. 1	28 " 3	28 " 7
29 Mark 1		29 " 16	29 " 2	29 " 4	29 " 8
30 " 2		30 1 Cor. 1	30 " 3	30 " 5	30 " 9
31 " 3		31 " 2		31 " 6	

CALENDAR.

July.		Aug.		Sept.		Oct.		Nov.		Dec.	
1	Gen. 10	1	Gen. 41	1	Ex. 22	1	Nu. 12	1	Deut. 7	1	Josh 3
2	" 11	2	" 42	2	" 23	2	" 13	2	" 8	2	" 4
3	" 12	3	" 43	3	" 24	3	" 14	3	" 9	3	" 5
4	" 13	4	" 44	4	" 25	4	" 15	4	" 10	4	" 6
5	" 14	5	" 45	5	" 26	5	" 16	5	" 11	5	" 7
6	" 15	6	" 46	6	" 27	6	" 17	6	" 12	6	" 8
7	" 16	7	" 47	7	" 28	7	" 18	7	" 13	7	" 9
8	" 17	8	" 48	8	" 29	8	" 19	8	" 14	8	" 10
9	" 18	9	" 49	9	" 30	9	" 20	9	" 15	9	" 11
10	" 19	10	" 50	10	" 31	10	" 21	10	" 16	10	" 12
11	" 20	11	Ex. 1	11	" 32	11	" 22	11	" 17	11	" 13
12	" 21	12	" 2	12	" 33	12	" 23	12	" 18	12	" 14
13	" 22	13	" 3	13	" 34	13	" 24	13	" 19	13	" 15
14	" 23	14	" 4	14	" 35	14	" 25	14	" 20	14	" 16
15	" 24	15	" 5	15	" 36	15	" 26	15	" 21	15	" 17
16	" 25	16	" 6	16	" 37	16	" 27	16	" 22	16	" 18
17	" 26	17	" 7	17	" 38	17	" 28	17	" 23	17	" 19
18	" 27	18	" 8	18	" 39	18	" 29	18	" 24	18	" 20
19	" 28	19	" 9	19	" 40	19	" 30	19	" 25	19	" 21
20	" 29	20	" 10	20	Num. 1	20	" 31	20	" 26	20	" 22
21	" 30	21	" 11	21	" 2	21	" 32	21	" 27	21	" 23
22	" 31	22	" 12	22	" 3	22	" 33	22	" 28	22	" 24
23	" 32	23	" 13	23	" 4	23	" 34	23	" 29	23	Ps. 135
24	" 33	24	" 14	24	" 5	24	" 35	24	" 30	24	" 136
25	" 34	25	" 15	25	" 6	25	" 36	25	" 31	25	" 144
26	" 35	26	" 16	26	" 7	26	Deut. 1	26	" 32	26	" 145
27	" 36	27	" 17	27	" 8	27	" 2	27	" 33	27	" 146
28	" 37	28	" 18	28	" 9	28	" 3	28	" 34	28	" 147
29	" 38	29	" 19	29	" 10	29	" 4	29	Josh. 1	29	" 148
30	" 39	30	" 20	30	" 11	30	" 5	30	" 2	30	" 149
31	" 40	31	" 21			31	" 6			31	" 150

142 THE PRAYER-MEETING.

And in connection with these daily readings of the Scripture the annexed list of topics for the fifty-two weekly prayer-meetings have been suggested for general use:

Jan. 1. The Temptation of Christ. Matt. 4:1-11.
" 2. Methods and Spirit of Prayer. Matt. 6:5-15.
" 3. Faith for Others. Matt. 15:21-28.
" 4. Consecration Tested. Matt. 19:16-20.
" 5. Jesus in Gethsemane. Matt. 26:30-36.
Feb. 1. Parable of the Sower. Mark 4:1-20.
" 2. The Demoniac Son Healed. Mark 9:14-29.
" 3. The Baptism of the Spirit. Acts 2:1-21.
" 4. Paul's Conversion. Acts 9:1-22.
Mar. 1. Divine Service. Acts 20:18-35.
" 2. Christian Enthusiasm. Acts 26:24, 25.
" 3. Assurance of Faith and Hope. Romans 8:28-39.
" 4. Consecration. Romans 12;1, 2.
" 5. Truth Revealed by the Spirit. 1 Cor. 2.
April 1. The Believer—God's Temple. 1 Cor. 3:9-17.
" 2. One Spirit—Diverse Gifts. 1 Cor. 12.
" 3. Weakness Made Strength. 2 Cor. 12:7-10.
" 4. Giving and Gaining. 2 Cor. 9.
May 1. Saved by Grace. Gal. 3:1-4.
" 2. The Christian Walk. Eph. 4:5.
" 3. Seeking the Prize. Phil. 3:7-15.
" 4. Resurrection Life. Col. 3:9-17.
" 5. The Comforting Hope. 1 Thess. 4:13-18.
June 1. Perilous Times. 2 Tim. 3:1-13.
" 2. Divine Sympathy and Succour. Heb. 4:15, 16.
" 3. Patience and Faith. Heb. 10:36-38.
" 4. Walking with God. Gen. 5:22.
July 1. The Bow in the Cloud. Gen. 9:13.
" 2. Intercession. Gen. 18:23-33.
" 3. The Lord will Provide. Gen. 22:14.

THE PRAYER-MEETING. 143

July 4. Prevailing Prayer. Gen. 32: 24–32.
" 5. The Lord in the Prison. Gen. 39: 21.
Aug. 1. Our Short-sightedness. Gen. 42: 36.
" 2. Faith and Worship. Ex. 4: 31.
" 3. The Covenant-Keeping God. Ex. 6: 2–8.
" 4. The Passover. Ex. 12.
Sept. 1. The Ten Commandments. Ex. 20: 1–17.
" 2. Holiness to the Lord. Ex. 28: 36–43.
" 3. The Lord's Presence. Ex. 33: 14–17.
" 4. The Cloud and the Glory. Ex. 40: 34–38.
Oct. 1. A Noble Example. Num. 11: 25–29.
" 2. The Smitten Rock. Num. 20: 8–12.
" 3. Baalim's Empty Wish. Num. 23: 10.
" 4. No Compromise. Num. 33: 50–56.
" 5. Only Take Heed. Deut. 4: 9, 10.
Nov. 1. God's Care of His People. Deut. 7: 6–17.
" 2. Love of God's Word. Deut. 11: 18–25.
" 3. Courage from God. Deut. 20: 1-8.
" 4. The First belongs to God. Deut. 26: 1-11.
" 5. Blessings upon Penitents. Deut. 30: 1-16.
Dec. 1. Result of Courage. Josh. 1: 5–18.
" 2. Victory from God. Josh. 6: 1-20.
" 3. Sin a Hindrance. Josh. 7: 6-26.
" 4. Cities of Refuge.
" 5. Praise. Psalms.

The adoption of such a plan as this would prove a powerful auxiliary to the daily cultivation of piety as set forth in our fourth chapter. And it has these conspicuous merits, that it secures uniformity, that the topics grow out of the daily readings, and that the daily readings prepare for the topics and help to illustrate them. All in all it is a most admirable combination that cannot fail to recommend its adoption to all who are earnestly praying for salvation in Israel and the more general establishment of our Redeemer's kingdom. Fly, O thou angel having in charge to preach the everlasting Gospel unto all them that dwell on the earth, and to every nation, and kindred and tongue and people, and say to them all, Fear God, honor and obey Him.

But whether we shall have uniform topics or not, either on a limited or a general scale, let us have interesting prayer-meetings. Let us set to work with such earnestness and let us adopt such methods as under the divine blessing shall secure them.

CHAPTER XVII.

HELPS TO SPEAKING IN PUBLIC.

Those who attempt to speak in public for the first time need to be told that the agitation of mind which often accompanies the effort is not peculiar to themselves, but is an experience common to all, or nearly so, and is not to be taken as a sign that they will never be able to speak with freedom and delight.

There may be some who are natural orators, born such, like the poet of whom Horace writes, and to such nothing need be said. They take to speaking as naturally as ducks to water. The perfect orator is one who knows everything, and is always prepared, knows just what to say, how to say it, and when to say it. His will power is so imperial that nothing can daunt or subdue it; against whom the storms of opposing faction beat in vain. His sensibilities are so tender that they are responsive to every emotion, and so deep as to impress every hearer. He is like the lake on whose surface every breeze makes an impression, and from whose depths the storms stir up the waves that sweep the sky and carry everything along with them. The trembling heart and the responsive eye give proper tones to expression and suitable look and gesture to every action.

The majority of mankind are less gifted and need to study and premeditate in order to know what to say; they need to practice in order to learn how best to say it, and by frequent trial on the waves of extempore speech acquire the secret of speaking with force, verve, precision and persuasion. If there is any comfort in that, there are many examples of those who at the outset have made miserable failures. The case of Sheridan is well known. His " maiden speech" in the House of Commons was a failure that nearly drove him wild, but not to despair; for he immediately vowed "that it was in him and should come out." He persevered and became one of the most brilliant orators in English history. The life of Disraeli, the present Earl Beaconsfield, furnishes an example exactly similar to that of Sheridan's. It is related of Livingstone, the African explorer, that the first time he tried to preach for a minister who was ill, he could get out nothing beyond the text, and after repeated trials he walked down the steps of the pulpit, took up his hat, and went away leaving sermon and service unfinished. It is said that when the poet Longfellow visited London, he accepted the compliment of a breakfast on the express condition that there should be no public speaking. But some clever man purposely laid a trap for him, got up and toasted him in some very complimentary remarks. These called for a response from the poet. In his embarrassment he arose, attempted a speech, but could get out nothing but something like this: "Gentlemen, I thank you." When Dr. Windship, the Yankee Hercules, first appeared with a lecture before a Boston audience to tell how he had acquired his immense strength, he was so overcome by the sight of his audience as to faint in their presence; but immediately upon recovering and learning the cause of his discomfiture, he said: "What! a man that can lift two thousand pounds afraid of an audience, impossible! Let me go before them again, I will and must tell them what I have to say"—and tell them he did. John Stuart Mill frequently halted in his speeches, and yet was a very forcible and clear speaker. But I need not multiply instances to prove that men of profound thought and great ability have experienced great difficulty in acquiring the habit of extempore speech.

The majority of those who have succeeded as public speakers, have taken considerable pains to perfect themselves in oratory. It is related of the Rev. Joseph Cook by those who know him intimately that even when a mere boy he liked nothing better than to go into the open air and speak extemporaneously on some random subject, and all through his course of study at the academy and college he gave particular attention to the practice of oratory. It is said that Henry Clay in early life practiced in a barn where the astonished cattle were his auditors. During many years Newman Hall spent fifteen minutes each day in the practice of extempore speech, and took his subject from whatever page of his Bible to which he opened at random. The example of Demosthenes is so often adduced as to be threadbare, but yet no example is more pertinent; for he has stood in all ages as the acknowledged master of eloquence. It was by the utmost diligence he became such. You will remember how he spoke before the waves of the surging sea, that the roar of a multitude might cease to be terrifying; you will remember how he overcame shortness of breath and an impediment in speech by running up hill and articulating words with pebbles in his mouth. Very pertinently has Cicero condensed an all-important rule for success into a threefold practice; for when asked, "What was the first requisite for oratory?" he replied,

"Action." "What is the second?" "Action." "What is the third?" "Action."

But as a general thing those who take part in a prayer-meeting do not contemplate the acquisition of oratory to the extent in which the masters of eloquence have acquired it; they will be content if they can speak upon a subject with comfort to themselves and edification to others, and offer prayer in such phrases as shall indicate their sincerity, and not show that they have more zeal than knowledge. Let us enumerate some principles that may serve as helps in this direction.

An excellent help will be to meditate frequently upon your subject, and even to pray over it. This will prove a suitable soil for the reception of your subject, out of which shall grow the tree of thought, with its fruit of forcible expression for public speech.

Then again talk about your subject with others. In efforts to explain it, suitable words will come, and with them a fuller understanding of the subject, and oft times new ideas from those with whom you converse. Such exercise, like the whirl of the sling before the stone is cast, or the bend of the bow before the arrow flies, will give momentum to your thought and send it to the brow of conviction.

And as you know what the subject will be on

which you desire to speak, gather up illustrations from your own experience, from your walks in daily life, from your work and business, and from the company you keep. Keep your eyes and ears open, and you will find "tongues in trees, books in the running brooks, sermons in stones, and good in everything." Truly the attentive listener will hear the grass grow, and at every step in life find illustrations that shall prove feathers to guide the arrow of discourse in its flight, and barbs to its head to make it stick.

It will be wise also to read on your subject. If you digest and assimilate what you read, this will enrich your own thought, and make what you shall say all the more valuable. It will also help you to more accurate expression in speech, if you write on your subject. "Reading maketh a full man, conference a ready man, and writing an exact man." But if you write, it should not be with a view to committing it to memory; for this will always keep you in bondage, and prevent you from acquiring the larger liberty of extempore speech. It was the maxim of Pultenay, the first Earl of Bath, that there are "few orators who commence with set speeches," and in practicing on this rule he became one of the leading speakers in Parliament.

And these various parts in preparation will prove so many steps by which your subject shall work itself down into your own heart. The home of eloquence is the heart; for like music, poetry and painting, oratory springs from the heart. "The greatest thoughts do not spring from the understanding, but enter into it from the heart of man; the heart is the bud of the head." To be devoid of feeling is to be devoid of eloquence. When we feel deeply, we think clearly, and talk freely. "If you wish me to weep," says Horace, "you must first weep yourself." "My heart was hot within me," says the Psalmist; "while I was musing the fire burned: then spake I with my tongue." So likewise Jeremiah: "But his word was in mine heart as a burning fire shut up in my bones, and I was weary with forbearing and I could not stay." Without heart in them, thoughts may be ever so clear, but they will be lacking in that warmth which eloquence engenders; they may dazzle, but they will come as cold as a beam of light from an iceberg.

Another excellent rule for speech in the prayer-meeting is this: be brief. This was Luther's suggestive maxim: "Get up boldly; open your mouth widely; be done quickly." If you set out to speak half an hour, you might find it very difficult to fill the time; but if you get up with something to say that you must say, born of such preparation as has been indicated, when you have poured out your thought, stop. When you are through, have done. There is many a man that does not know when to stop, but flies like a wounded bird from bush to bush till he drops by sheer exhaustion. John Bright, "the great commoner," when interviewed said, "the only part of my speech that I prepare in set words is the conclusion. I always know how and when I am going to stop." Be content to say a few things well, rather than many poorly. When it shall become the rule to speak as briefly as possible, we shall find that we have more to say than we thought we had, that it is easier to speak than we thought it was, and that what we say goes straighter to the mark than we thought it would.

And with reference to prayer, the same rules apply as to speaking. Be brief in your petitions, seek the guidance of the Spirit in the effort, pray in the family and in the closet, and thus your voice in prayer will not sound strange to your ears, and prove mere words of the mouth rather than those which have their source in the heart. Have some purpose in your prayer, something to ask for, something to rejoice over, and something to give thanks for. Study the models of prayer to be found in the Bible and seek to enter into the spirit of their petitions.

A full and comprehensive prayer may include: "Adoring the glory and perfection of God; giving thanks to him for all his mercies, general and particular, spiritual and temporal, common and special, above all, for Christ Jesus, his unspeakable gift, and the hope of eternal life through him; making humble confession of sin and earnest supplication for the pardon of sin, for peace with God, and for the fruit of the Spirit; pleading from every principle warranted in Scripture, from our necessity, and the all-sufficiency of God; and intercession for others, the growth of the church, the welfare of society, and the urgent interests of that community to which we immediately belong." But every prayer need not include all these particulars, as is evident from the prayers of Scripture; but such parts as our immediate object in prayer may require. For the Bible gives us three classes of models: first, those that are very brief, hardly more than a sentence, like the publican's prayer; second, those of medium length, like the "Lord's Prayer;" and third, those of greater length, like the prayer of dedication by Solomon, the confession and prayer of Daniel,—or the high-priestly prayer of the Lord.

But whatever be the result of your attempts to speak in public, do not be discouraged. Do not be prevented from having your say, though your mind be agitated, and the trepidation promises to stick by you through life. The agitation of your mind may arise from constitutional peculiarities. It is difficult to control one's temperament and compel shaking knees to stand still. But this will prove no serious hindrance to your success as a speaker, if you will only accept it as a fact, and press forward with invincible resolution. Cicero has said of himself, that "he grew pale at the beginning of a speech, and felt a tremor in every part of his frame." And of his first attempt he said, " I was so intimidated, that (I speak it with the highest sense of gratitude) Quintus Maximus adjourned the Court, when he perceived me thus oppressed and disabled with concern." Nor are some of the bravest and boldest ministers, who have seen years of service, strangers to this perturbation. " I am now an old man," said Luther, " and have been a long while occupied in preaching; but I never ascend the pulpit without a tremor."

It is a twice-told tale. There are none who cannot become forcible speakers, if they set out with a determination to conquer, if it takes all summer. "The gods sell us every thing for labor," says an old Greek proverb. Intelligent and continuous practice will achieve success and produce a certain measure of freedom. Perhaps the example of Mr. Moody is as good as any that can be found in the way of encouragement. One could hardly have more obstacles in the way than he had. Mr. William Reynolds, of Peoria, related the following interesting reminiscence at a convention held in Canada three or four years ago: "The first meeting I ever saw him at, was in a little old shanty that had been abandoned by a saloon-keeper. Mr. Moody had got the place to hold a meeting in at night. I went there a little late; and the first thing I saw was a man standing up, with a few tallow candles around him, holding a negro boy, and trying to read to him the story of the Prodigal Son; and a great many of the words he could not make out, and had to skip. I thought, if the Lord can ever use such an instrument as that for His honor and glory, it will astonish me. After that meeting was over Mr. Moody said to me, 'Reynolds, I have got only one talent: I have no education, but I love the Lord Jesus Christ, and I want to do something for Him; and I want you to pray for me.' I have never ceased from that day to this, morning and night, to pray for that devoted Christian soldier. I have watched him since then, have had counsel with him, and know him thoroughly; and for consistent walk and conversation I have never met a man to equal him. It astounds me when I look back and see what Mr. Moody was thirteen years ago, and then what he is under God to-day—shaking Scotland to its very centre, and reaching now over to Ireland. The last time I heard from him, his injunction was, 'Pray for me every day; pray now that God will keep me humble.'"

Public speaking at the outset may prove like the efforts of a boy learning to skate. It is attended with many a fall and bruise; but presently that which in the beginning was so slow and dangerous, becomes safe and delightful. How well I remember what a pleasure skating became after I had learned how to skate. With what bounding joy I rushed forward, the moment I caught sight of the river, with what eager haste I buckled on my skates, and with what ecstacy of delight I flew away over the frozen field as it lay beneath my feet like a mirror glittering in the sun—" it was a thing of beauty and a joy forever."

Is not the experience of Mr. Moody something like this? It cannot now be otherwise than the greatest joy for him to speak with such freedom, power, and perfect command of himself and his audience. Be content to fail a number of times, if that is necessary, but " don't give up the ship." Be encouraged by his noble example, and no longer let " I dare not wait upon I would: "

> "I would, but cannot sing,
> I would, but cannot pray,"
> I would, but cannot speak.

With reasonable effort and perseverance, we shall conquer a reasonable and enjoyable fluency in speech and prayer—not for its own sake, but that as living witnesses to the power of truth, God may take our words and make them suitable instruments of persuasion to the edification of the church, the conversion of sinners, and the advancement of His Kingdom.

CHAPTER XVIII.

How to Secure Attendance.

In many of our churches there is the largest attendance in the morning; the evening service is left to take care of itself. And if this is so for the Sabbath, what shall we say for the prayer-meeting? The audience rooms of the churches are all too large, and only those are used for the Wednesday evening meetings where no lecture-rooms are attached. The prayer-meeting in the main room of the church would simply be lost, and the leader, like Diogenes, would have to take a lantern in order to hunt up the people and find where to stand while conducting the exercises.

This statement is as true for England as for America. Let us adduce testimony. "How are the prayer-meetings almost universally neglected!" says Spurgeon. "Our own church stands out like an almost solitary green islet in the midst of a dark, dark, sea; one bright pearl in the depths of an ocean of discord and confusion. Look at the neighboring churches. Step into the vestry, and see a smaller band of people than you would like to think of, assembled around the pastor, whose heart is dull and heavy. Hear one brother after another pour out the dull, monotonous prayer that he has said by heart these fifty years; and then go away and say: 'Where is the spirit of prayer, where the life of devotion?' Is it not almost extinct? Are not our churches 'fallen, fallen, fallen from their high estate?' God wake them up, and send them more earnest and praying men!"

But, if it is the duty of the pastor to preach on Sabbath evenings, is it not the duty of the church to attend? Is there more room than they can fill? Then why did they build the church too large? If it is the duty of the church to have a prayer-meeting, is it not the duty of all the church members to attend and do their best to make it as successful as possible?

In a few churches, very happily, there are found the "sons of thunder" to fill them with their eloquence, and the question with them is not how to make the people attend, but how to let them in and make room for them. Now these men of fire will play around the gilt rods of the highest steeples, and those who live in provincial towns, on the heath or in the backwoods need not look for such displays to fill their houses. Let them accept the situation and be content with such good men as the Lord shall be pleased to send them. The people are not helpless; if they will only set to work, what is to prevent them from filling the lecture-room and the church on every occasion? There is nothing at all. "Let us go up at once, and possess it; for we are well able to overcome it." In God's name and with God's help let us hold and occupy the field. If eloquence is lacking, if fine music is lacking; let us fall back upon the good old Gospel and our own duties under it. But be well assured, if you allow one-half or one-third of the church to perform all the duties of the church, there is but a small blessing in store for your church. "Curse ye Meroz, said the angel of the Lord, curse ye bitterly the inhabitants thereof; because they came not to the help of the Lord, to the help of the Lord against the mighty."

If we cannot make the evening attendance on the church and the prayer-meeting a self-executing privilege let us bring it into the domain of duty. With this end in view let the people pledge themselves to attend. Let a covenant be prepared to emphasize the importance of a full attendance in such terms as shall meet the exigencies of the case, and then let some judicious persons take it around among the people for signatures. After these have been secured, the pastor can have the pledge printed on a card and a copy returned to each signer with a brief letter exhorting each to keep in mind what has been pledged, and to seek divine guidance in its full performance.

Let us sketch an outline of such a pledge:

We, the undersigned, do each and severally covenant together, that the work of God may not suffer from our neglect, to faithfully, regularly and punctually attend all the public services of the church on Sabbath morning and evening, and also and especially the meeting for prayer on the week-day evening. We agree that the only excuses for non-attendance shall be such as will approve themselves to our conscience at the time, and as we trust will pass muster on the great review day above.

We also promise to study the topic for the prayer-meeting, and take such part in its social worship as our duty shall indicate. We are God's witnesses, and as such we desire to speak and pray that eventually our duty may prove a pleasure and participation more a privilege than an unwelcome burden. But whether we take part or not, we will not forsake "the assembling of ourselves" together, as has been the manner of some from the beginning, unless unavoidable circumstances prevent us from meeting with the brethren in public assembly.

We also promise that we will not only come ourselves, but also by the grace of God helping us, we will invite and endeavor to bring others with us, that thus the rooms of the church may be filled and the rich blessings of God's love and mercy may be as widely distributed in our community as possible (Rev. 22:17).

And we also promise that if we are absent from any stated meeting we shall always be ready to speak to our pastor or our brethren in the Lord about such absence, and that any inquiry into our excuses by them shall not give us offence, but be thankfully received by us and esteemed one of the means whereby to provoke unto love and good works.

All this we covenant and agree in the sight of God, who reads our hearts and will approve or condemn our motives according as He sees them to be sincere or not.

SIGNED, ...

In this matter we need to carry the standard pretty well up to the front. And no one need doubt but that such fidelity in the discharge of duties as this would secure among all the members would soon fill the church, and wonderfully stimulate the Christian zeal of all in a community. In one of the fierce battles in the South, so it is related, a colored soldier stood with the banner well up in the front. An officer, fearing that the ensign would be captured, cried out in the thick of the fight, "Come back with that flag!" "Massa, cap'n," the dusky hero replied, "this yeah flag never go back; bring up dem men dar!" "Dem men dar" came up to the support of their colors, and turned the tide of defeat into a well-earned victory.

My Christian brother, carry the standard well up to the front, and then bring up those non-attending and nomadic members from the fields, the woods, and the rear, into rank and file, around the uplifted standard of the Cross—and who has ever rallied round an ensign more glorious and inspiring?—and the tide of battle will be successfully turned into a victory for every church that is now feeble and despondent. Come to the prayer-meeting whether you take part or not. There may be sufficient reason for your silence, but you can always speak by your presence. To be always at the prayer-meeting is an action as eloquent as any speech.

Let church attendance be the last active out-door duty from which you will retire. Have a resolute mind and an unconquerable spirit, and you will live all the longer for such activity; and what is more, you will enjoy your old age, and we shall hear little about your influence being lost, and you yourself laid on the shelf. Old age need not and should not come to thee to wither up thy faculties, and make thy days long and wearisome. In attendance on the prayer-meeting be as hale and tough as old hickory. Just here we happen to know what can be done if there be first the willing and decisive mind. We know an entire family that during two years lived six miles from church, and yet they regularly attended the prayer-meeting, driving twelve miles to do so, in summer as in winter, in moonshine as in darkness, over a dangerous road. But you live six blocks from church, and call it far! Simeon and Anna, when we read of them, were very old, yet their daily attendance on the temple at morning and evening sacrifice ceased not on that account. Simeon doubtless found it a trial on his strength to go up the hill to the top of Moriah, where stood the glorious temple of God; and it may be that Anna found it a sort of self-denial to continue in the temple, serving "God with fastings and prayers night and day;" but, O how precious was their reward! Ere they withdrew from active life, they were both permitted to see the Lord's Anointed, to hold him lovingly in their arms, and to speak of him " to all them that looked for redemption in Jerusalem."

There are many in our churches—and it is delightful to see them—who are as regular as the seasons in attendance upon the public services of God's house. They have a place there, and are always in it, irrespective of the weather,—may their tribe increase. If you look for them in their place and see them not, you are either growing blind or something like a land-slide has taken place between their house and the church.

And perhaps it will not be out of place to give just one instance of the working of the pledge for church

THE PRAYER-MEETING.

and prayer-meeting attendance. It is done with no intention of finding fault with the church that originated the method, but rather to hold them up as an example of great wisdom, and, under the circumstances, to praise them for the important discovery they have made. "The Calvary Presbyterian Church" of Springfield, Mo., is the leading church in its Presbytery, and well-known for its labors of love and self-sacrifice; but its members had fallen into the habit so common in all our city churches, of absenting themselves from the evening services in considerable numbers. Their pastor-elect, in this view of the case, felt it to be his duty to resign. But the church would not permit this, and especially so when they learned the reason. They called a meeting of the congregation and immediately applied a remedy for nonattendance in the shape of a pledge which was drawn up and signed: it was handed to the pastor, and of course the ground of his action was removed. He then prefixed a letter to the pledge and had both printed together on a card, so that a copy might be sent to each one of the original signers. The following is a literal copy of that card:

"Brethren, be not weary in well-doing."

Dear ....

The following Pledge was handed to me with your name signed to it. The good Lord is pleased with our vows made to Him, when He sees us earnestly trying to keep them. Believing that a frequent reading of this solemn Pledge to which you have subscribed your name will assist you to carry it out, I herewith send you a copy of it. Please read Psalm lxvi., 12; Psalm lxxvi., 11; Psalm cxvi., 14.

Your Pastor,
C. H. DUNLAP.

PLEDGE.

We now pledge ourselves to self-examination and prayer, that the Holy Spirit may come into our hearts; to seek His enlightening power, that we may see our duty as believers, and to impart to us such a sense of our obligations to our Lord as will enable us to engage heartily in all Christian work, by a more regular attendance upon all the services of the sanctuary, by the cultivation of the grace of benevolence, and by seeking such a spirit of love to all that we shall set a watch upon our lips and hearts, that all evil speaking, with all bitterness, may be put away from us.

"Lo! I am with you always."

"Forsake not the assembling of yourselves together."

"Whatsoever thy hand findeth to do, do it with thy might."

So far as we know, the result of this action has come up to their most sanguine expectations. The evening services were at once well attended, the pastor was greatly encouraged—for to preach to slim audiences in the evening is the severest trial of the pastor's duty—the people were delighted by the new tokens of refreshing from the presence of the Lord, and with increased hopefulness the work began to go forward in their midst. Both pastor and people are entitled to honorable mention for having so happily and harmoniously solved the difficulty, and their discovery is one that should not be lost to the church at lage.

"Examine yourselves, whether ye be in the faith; prove your own selves, how that Jesus Christ is in you, except ye be reprobates."—2 Cor. 13: 5.

CHAPTER XIX.

How Prayer-Meetings are kept at a White Heat.

"How are prayer-meetings kept at a white heat?"—*Correspondent.*

To answer the above question in a very practical way, we detailed a ministerial reporter to visit several of the most successful prayer-meetings in New York and Brooklyn. We transfer the following from his note-book:

At Fulton Street noon-day prayer-meeting, which has met every business day at noon for the past twenty years, we found in attendance about one hundred people, mostly business men. The meeting began punctually at 1 o'clock to the minute. No speech or prayer was allowed to exceed five minutes. A portion of Scripture, carefully prepared by a previously appointed leader, was read and commented on very briefly and pointedly. Requests for prayer, twenty or thirty, were read from the desk, others were made verbally by speakers. Prayers were earnest. Every minute was occupied. No loud talking, noise or excitement, but the deepest kind of earnestness was manifested. The assembly had the appearance of a meeting of a lot of earnest business men who had come together to talk over some vital business matter. The leading spirits of this meeting are men of conviction; men who are as sure God answers prayer as they are that the sun is shining above the clouds at noon to-day. Promptness, eagerness, earnestness, common business sense applied to religion, faith, and the consequent presence of the Spirit of God, keep this meeting at " white heat."

The prayer-meeting at the Brooklyn tabernacle is, perhaps, more largely attended than any other in the world. We found about two thousand people in attendance; it was a threefold meeting, and lasts from 7½ to 9¼ o'clock. The first half hour is spent in congregational singing—singing the hymns for the following services: (This church has no choir, but is led in its singing by the organ and a precentor) From 8 to 8½ o'clock, Dr. Talmage delivers a prepared and, to his audience, an exceedingly interesting " review of the secular events of the week from a religious standpoint." This review is gotten up in a popular lecture style, and helps to draw the crowds. At the conclusion of the lecture the audience has permission to retire or remain for the prayer-meeting proper. The lecture bait has evidently caught many. Curiosity is excited, so the larger proportion of the great audience remain. Dr. Talmage takes his seat on the front of the platform and calls upon some brother, who has the gift to make a brief, earnest, sympathetic prayer, to pray. The leader keeps the reins well in hand: "I would like to take testimony to-night whether Christianity is true or not. The Bible says that those who are faithful Christians will know that Christianity is true. There are those here whom you know to be honest men; men who would scorn to bear false testimony. They have been Christians for twenty, thirty, fifty years. Now, what say they? Do they know by experience that Christianity is a truth? You would take their testimony on any other matter. There is no judge in this city who would not deem them capable witnesses. Here is a matter of which they say they have positive knowledge. They are capable witnesses." One after another of aged Christians was called upon to bear testimony concerning his experimental knowledge of the truth of the religion of Jesus. Younger men testified. Brief exhortations by the pastor, and others in the same line of thought followed. Prayers, pointed and brief, were made for the immediate conversion of the unconverted present. Then, those desiring the prayers of God's people were requested to stand up. Fifty or more arose. After an earnest prayer by the pastor, the meeting adjourned. The prayer-meeting proper lasted three-quarters of an hour.

Here also they have found the secret of keeping a prayer-meeting at "white heat."

—*Metropolitan Pulpit.*

CHAPTER XX.

Treatment of the Monthly Concert.

The Gospel needs of the world are so great and important, that a place for their consideration ought to be given them in the scheme of topics. Now it is so well known that the monthly concert for missions will be a dry presentation of facts and figures, that people more readily stay away on those evenings than any other. We have only to improve this treatment and make it pleasing, as well as instructive, in order to arouse the attention of the church and secure fuller attendance.

We have already adverted to a general plan by which the concert can be made more interesting than it usually is, but some additional particulars may here be specified which shall give a growing interest to the monthly presentation of the missionary subjects.

The concert should be made the occasion for the study of history. I suppose none of us know too much about the history of lands other than our own. Each month we have a particular field under view. Let us investigate certain subjects connected with the history of that portion of the world, such as its lan-

THE PRAYER-MEETING. 173

guage, literature, religion, social condition, and political relations. Let us take India, for example. We may profitably study from year to year such subjects as these: The history of India from the earliest times; the importance of the discovery of the new way to India by the Cape of Good Hope; the chartering of the East India Company by Queen Elizabeth; the licence granted to this company by the Great Mogul to establish a trading-post in India; the steps by which this populous and extended region was opened for the Gospel; the rule of the East India Company; the impeachment of Warren Hastings; how was their opposition to the spread of the Gospel finally overcome? the struggle over renewal of charter in 1813; the Crimean War and its results; the Sepoy Rebellion; the extinction of the Company's rule and the elevation of Victoria as sovereign of India in 1858; her elevation to be Empress of India in 1877; the civilization of India under British rule; the labors of this and that missionary in India, etc.

Nor will it be out of place to devote time to the study of geography in its two branches of physical and descriptive—the climate and the products of the soil in their relation to civilization and religion—hindrances in the way of civilizing Africa from climate—is not a more moderate or colder climate more favorable?—the explorations and discoveries of Livingstone and Stanley in Africa—physical geography as modified by human action. Thus in China, at the present, the lamentable famine by which thousands are perishing has been caused by the destruction of the forests in that sadly-stricken region. In former times, the hills which "fringe that vast plateau, now the seat of famine, were covered with thick woods. They have been entirely cleared. From Pekin to Hankow, a distance of 700 miles, scarcely a tree or shrub is to be seen." As a result of such wasteful destruction, 70,000,000 of people in this thickly settled region are in want of food, and some 9,000,000 of them are actually starving. This is a lesson that should not be lost on the people of the United States. "Woodman, spare that tree."

Again, the concert will give excellent opportunity for the study of comparative religion. There are about a dozen different religions of mankind. What are the distinctive features of each? Five of these, for example, are found in India—Brahminism, Mohammedanism, Buddhism, Chrstianity and Parseeism. The three essentially missionary religions of the world—Christianity, Mohammedanism and Buddhism—are here confronting each other, and struggling for supremacy. What will be the result? By methods of research like these, we shall become better acquainted with the moral condition of the great un-

THE PRAYER-MEETING. 175

christian world, and the churches will be progressively enlightened about its immediate and pressing needs.

And finally, a brief presentation of what is being accomplished yearly in each field will be useful to awaken an interest and give it intelligent direction; and from such knowledge of struggles and hindrances, defeats and triumphs, hopes and encouragements, the church will learn better both how to pray and how to contribute.

The annual recurrence of the same missionary fields should not call for a repetition of the same thoughts, but should afford the occasion for the progressive presentation of new lines in history, religion, geography, government and achievements. To revive a missionary zeal in the churches, we need only to pour in a flood of light upon these subjects, and as a result, under the divine blessing, such a prayerful interest will be maintained in the world-wide diffusion of the Gospel as shall advance the cause of truth both at home and abroad.

> " Watchman, tell me does the morning
>   Of fair Zion's glory dawn;
> Have the signs that mark His coming
>   Yet upon my pathway shone?
> Pilgrim, yes, arise, look round thee,
>   Light is breaking in the skies;
> Spurn the unbelief that bound thee,
>   Morning dawns, arise, arise!"

CHAPTER XXI.

Laying Out Work.

It has been claimed by an English clergyman,* that the church of to-day has lost its early and practical character, and hence fails to accomplish her full work. He objects that it is all preaching and no work. "The kind of meeting to which this pointed (Heb. 10: 24, 25) was a meeting in which everybody who chose had a voice, in which everybody who had any advice or information or exhortation to give was free to give, and was expected to give it." "To provoke unto love and good works," to consider one another, to take steps for the relief of their poor, the succor of their sick, the instruction of the young, the conversion of their heathen friends, the advancement of their faith, the promotion of every scheme which an enthusiastic philanthropy suggested for making the world better and happier,—this was the business which brought them together. They did not meet as we do to sing psalms, pray and hear a sermon, and go

---

*Rev. J. Service.

away home till next Sunday. Their meetings did not end as ours regularly and systematically do, in nothing at all. And so, he reasons, we ought to introduce a more popular and practical element into our service. "If we were united," he goes on to say, "in the loosest sort of way, united as a congregation in an endeavor to further Christian objects, to relieve the poor, to comfort the sick, to instruct the ignorant, to reclaim the erring, to remove temptation out of the way of the young, to promote decency, sobriety, honesty, truth, gentleness,—if we were ever so loosely united as a congregation in this endeavor, it is impossible, being as many as we are, that we should not accomplish something. Now if there were this kind of business first, and devotion followed, or if business and devotion were somehow combined in the order of our Sunday services, we should have what gives zest to meetings for other and inferior purposes,—the sense that we are dealing with what is immediate and of practical utility to ourselves and others. Were we able to report to-day that some work for the poor, or the sick, or the ignorant, or the tempted had been done by us since last Sunday, or had we now met to spend part of our time in considering what work of that kind might be attempted by us this week, I need not say our meeting would be more lively, for one thing, than our meetings usually are, and not the least so in respect of our devotion. In carrying on our work the practical and useful would come to the aid of devotion; devotion would aid work; we should meet difficulties, and pray the better on account of them; we should have some success, and because of it sing a more hearty song." This he contends was the purpose for which the primitive Christians came together on the first day of the week, and this was the nature of their worship—a meeting in which all had a voice for the transactions of business, for reporting what had been done and for suggesting what might be done on the coming week; and hence they were so successful and grew in number so rapidly.

Now this criticism might be more applicable to a church which held no week-day meetings for conference, prayer and exhortation, without a Sabbath school, and with a changing congregation. We are thankfully to receive every suggestion that might aid a church to do more than it is doing for Christ and humanity—and there is probably no church but might do a little more than it is doing—but with the various meetings and schools which we have, there is less occasion for any change in the order and nature of our public services on the Sabbath. The church is a continuous organization and does not pass out of existence when her members go home to dine, or when the doors are closed at night for another week. And there is not so much change in the congregation either, except in the larger cities; so that the great majority of our churches are continuous organizations for work. We have the Sabbath school for instruction and a more intimate acquaintance with the facts and principles of the Bible. There remains, then, a need for just such pulpit ministrations as are now given on the Lord's Day, that thus the Spirit of God may make " the preaching of the Word an effectual means of convincing and converting sinners, and of building them up in holiness and comfort, through faith, unto salvation."

In some churches there are industrial schools where the young are regularly instructed in certain departments of home work, in neatness and cleanliness, and when cases of want and distress occur, they are looked after and relieved, and not only kind words are spoken, but also something to wear is given.

In most churches the ladies meet weekly from house to house for prayer and conference. The neighbors are invited in to participate, and in this way strangers are reached and new opportunities for doing good are discovered. And then there are the weekly prayer-meetings of the church, which present abundant opportunity for doing just such work, or planning for it, as was suggested for the Sunday service, and which, it seems to us, is more appropriate for such a time and meeting.

We might, perhaps, with great advantage to ourselves, introduce this feature into our prayer-meetings for a few minutes, or so many as should be needed, might be allotted for this purpose towards the close of the meeting, in which members might report what Christian work they had done, or were doing, whether they had been helpful to any, or had tried to be, to relieve the poor, to comfort the sick, to reclaim the erring, to remove temptation from the young, to promote the many good works for lack of which humanity lies suffering and bleeding, and to suggest what might be done while the week is still in progress; for in all these respects the church may prove herself a power for good in every community, and a fountain from which shall flow streams of blessing, sweetness and kindness. But in recounting work of this kind it would be very needful—and one could not be too careful,—to avoid the Pharisaic spirit, as illustrated by the parable of the Pharisee and the Publican, Luke 18: 9-14. But when the Christian is eaten up with zeal for the Lord's house and the Lord's work, he will run to and fro on the

Lord's business and esteem the service a gladsome privilege.

There are also other branches for beneficence in the machinery of the church—wheels within wheels—such as missionary bands, societies and officers in the church. These are set as watchmen upon the walls of our church that they may more readily discern what is useful and needful to do and to be done. We cannot, then, with so many arms and hands for work, complain of their lack, but rather of our failure to reach them out in as many helpful directions as the suffering needs of humanity require. Yes, the church is an organization for work. We are to be helpful to one another both spiritually and temporally. The church is the grandest of all organizations, because it is the body of Christ; and if there is any society that claims to be useful, the church should be all that and more.

We should have a watchful interest in each other, in the children and youth of the congregation, and ever seek to improve them, ever seek to help them in honorable and needful ways, so that they may be able to help themselves, and in their turn to be able to help others. When any one is out of employment and in need of place and work, we should be ready with kind words, hopeful sympathy and actual solicitation in their behalf. The true economy of life is to help others in such a way that they can help themselves. It is not so much charity they need as work and compensation.

Now it may be easier to send your money to the heathen, and delegate others to do good for you, than to take such personal interest in those right about you, that when they are in pressing need their wants shall receive immediate attention. And so it is reported of a wealthy firm in one of the great cities of the land, the members of which are pillars in a church—whose integrity no man questions—that they had had a man in their service until he became old and sick, and being unable to work, they stopped his salary, and he and his family were brought to the verge of starvation. Their attention was called to his condition, and a few dollars were sent for his relief; but it was a mere mite in contrast wih their munificent contributions to the charities of their church; and had it not been for the aid and sympathy of his fellow-clerks, he would have died, and received burial as a pauper. As it was, through their benevolence, the old man was supported comfortably while he lived, and in death received those kindly attentions which the heart loves to bestow on the objects of its care. The giving of large sums of money to a public charity attracts more notice and gains more fame than giving it for the benefit of some poor gamin—some Peter, John, or Paul—that has fallen among thieves on the road to Jericho. While so much money is sent to the bushmen of Africa or elsewhere, is there no one to take a personal interest in the tramp on the road to Jericho, the roustabout on a Mississippi steamer, the waif of the street whose home is a dry-goods box, or the orphan that sweeps the crossings, and begs a penny from my lord or lady as they pass on dry-shod and unsoiled. It is so much easier to weep over pictured misery in the South Sea Islands, than shed tears over the boot-black in your own city, whose scant earnings may buy bread and butter for some invalid mother or destitute sister. We all need to read and lay to heart the Parable of the Good Samaritan (Luke 10: 30–37).

The prayer-meeting will afford excellent opportunity to speak of just such cases as need help, work and sympathy. But if it be not proper to make such business a part of its exercises, it certainly will not be out of place to spend five or ten minutes after the close of each meeting in social intercourse about such charitable work as the church ought to undertake and prosecute. How easy it would be in this way to engender and stimulate a zeal for the thorough visitation of the district in which the church is located, in order to discover both the temporal and the spiritual wants of the neighboring community. How easy it would be to create an enthusiasm in works of benevolence, if such opportunity were given in connection with the discovery of wants and the comparison of notes. How easy it would be to fill up our churches, our Sabbath-schools and our prayer-meetings. It is not the ability that we lack, so much as the inclination and the zeal. God will give all the grace that such undertakings require as fast as the grace He has already given is used. Look at the zeal of Moody when a young convert. "His first effort was to hire four pews in Plymouth Church, Chicago, and keep them full of young men every Sunday;" and then next, to fill up a mission school on the North Side, and he has kept at this business of filling up churches ever since.

"Then shall the King say unto them on his right hand, Come, ye blessed of my Father, inherit the kingdom prepared from the foundation of the world: for I was an hungered and ye gave me meat; I was thirsty, and ye gave me drink: I was a stranger and ye took me in; naked and ye clothed me; I was sick and ye visited me; I was in prison and ye came unto me. Then shall the righteous answer him, saying Lord, when saw we thee an hungered, and fed thee? or thirsty and gave thee drink? When saw we thee a stranger, and took thee in? Or naked and clothed thee? or when saw we thee sick, or in prison, and came unto thee? And the King shall answer and say unto them, Verily I say unto you, inasmuch as ye have done it unto one of the least of these my brethren, ye have done it unto me."—Matt. 25: 34—40.

CHAPTER XXII.

Hints New and Old.

The following hints have been selected by way of review, and to emphasize some things of chief value to be looked after in the conduct of the prayer-meeting. "To every man his work." "England expects every man to do his duty." "Go work to-day in my vineyard."

I. Attendance, &c.

1. Arrange your affairs so as to attend the prayer-meeting, and be sure to come, unless under the same circumstances you would have to break a social or business engagement.

2. Come yourself. Bring your children. "The prayer-meeting is not complete without the children, any more than the family circle."

3. If you are entertaining friends, bring your visitors with you, and let the church give them a rousing social welcome after the meeting is closed.

4. Bring some unconverted friend with you, and pray for a blessing upon him before the meeting closes.

THE PRAYER-MEETING. 187

5. Come early, if possible; if not, come late; but by all means come early.

6. Come to the meeting in the spirit of prayer, and with the desire to take a part, should time and opportunity be given. "Those meetings have been the best that have been preceded by the most prayer."

7. Let the seats in front and near the leader be taken first. Sit side by side, and if there are to be any vacant chairs, let them be in the rear of the room. There is no rule for the success of religious meetings that Christians are slower to act upon than this—always to fill the front seats first and closely pack them. It seems a trivial thing, but it is a matter of prime importance. What kind of sociability would there be in a house if a dozen guests should sit down each in a room by himself, and then try to talk and be social through the doors and across the hall. Scatter the embers and they go out; draw them together and they burn and glow. The fingers in a mitten warm each other; in a glove they are chilled by separation.

8. Never give a concert, lecture, or other entertainment the preference if they come on the same evening as the prayer-meeting. Let the prayer-meeting be first.

9. Study and pray over the topic for the week,

that you may fill your mind with its precious truth, and make the prayer-meeting itself a theme of frequent conversation with your family and friends during the week.

10. Open and close the meeting promptly. If any indulgence is to be made, let it be in favor of a shorter rather than a longer session.

11. Occasionally devote five minutes or so at the close of the meeting for reports on work, or for new plans for work. There should also be an opportunity given somewhere in every meeting for a man to speak or pray whose heart is full and must find utterance, whether he is down on the programme or not.

12. Carefully exclude controversy and contradiction. The prayer-meeting is not a debating society.

13. As the weekly prayer-meeting is the gathering together of the household of Christ for growth in grace, for worship, and for mutual sympathy, let all restraint, formality and criticism be left outside. Don't let them cross the threshold. See Heb. 4 : 16.

14. But if all your efforts to wake up the mind of the church to the importance of prompt and full attendance on the prayer-meeting should fail, introduce the "League and Covenant" for attendance; and if that will not secure the hoped-for result, you

may conclude that you have sufficient reason as pastor to seek a different field of labor.

II. Variety.

In order not to have any monotony in the exercises from week to week, it will be wise to change them, and to a certain extent have the meetings, as they proceed, vary as to their nature. We place here what has previously been given on this head.

1. Conduct the meeting in the usual way. Custom has endeared it, and it may be really valuable.

2. If the topic be suitable, use it as the theme for a Bible reading.

3. Have a set programme, in which you have a place for one or two old men, for one or two middle-aged men, and for one or two young men, who have promised to attend and speak to the topic. Arrange also for two or three to pray for some urgent want of the church and congregation.

4. Announce for the next meeting that everything shall be voluntary, and just as soon as the topic has been developed, and the supply of participants ceases, stop the meeting, though you are but half through the hour; at all events, don't run beyond the time.

5. If you have a missionary topic, arrange for the reading of several letters, essays, etc.

6. If the season be suitable, arrange for a praise meeting, a promise meeting, a seed-time meeting, a "harvest-home" meeting, a memorial or Ebenezer meeting, and the like.

7. Occasionally have a new leader conduct the meeting. Such variety as this would introduce into the meetings would give life, animation and interest to them. The people would assemble each time in expectation of something new, and in this would not be disappointed.

III. *Procedure.*

1. "How is it then, brethren, when ye come together?" "Let everything be done unto edifying."

2. How can we cherish a sense of the Divine Presence in every meeting? Do we expect Christ to meet with us? How can we secure the aid and co-operation of the Holy Spirit, for without Him our meeting will be in vain, and worse than in vain? As aids to an answer, we ought to read, ponder and pray over such texts of Scripture as these: Matt. 18: 19, 20; Hos. 10: 12; Hab. 3: 2; Zech. 4: 6; Mark 1: 24; Rom. 8: 26, 27; Eph. 5: 18; Jas. 5: 16; and Luke 11: 19–13. Ought not the prayers, then, at the opening of the meeting to be burdened with petitions that God will hear us and grant us the presence of His Son and His Spirit?

3. Brevity in remarks and prayers is essential both to the interest of the meeting and its prompt dismissal. It is well to have as large a number as possible participate, so that, while the exercises have unity, they may not lack variety. Lengthy remarks generally become prosy, and long prayers are a departure from the models given in the Bible. The prayer of Solomon at the dedication of the temple— perhaps the longest prayer in the Bible—did not occupy much over five minutes. "But when ye pray, use not vain repetitions as the heathen do: for they think that they shall be heard for their much speaking." Experience has shown that from three to five minutes, on an average, is as much time as each one ought to use in taking part; and hence an address should make up in quality for what it lacks in quantity. Brevity will require condensation, point and application to our petitions, and unction in our devotion.

4. When you speak or pray, be sure to speak loud enough for all to hear you.

5. Inasmuch as in some of the denominations the ladies are silent, except as heard in song, why may not such present their thoughts from time to time in brief essays, to be read by the pastor or some of the brethren in the prayer-meeting? Such a custom in

these churches would tend to cultivate the various orders of Christian talent, and give us the benefit of womanly prudence, piety and wisdom.

6. Ought not "scolding" to be carefully avoided? Does it pay to scold those who are present, because others are absent? I know of a case where the church was just emptied by a minister scolding those who came because others kept away. If things do not go right, take them to the Lord in prayer. That will kindle a fire in the pulpit, that will kindle a fire in the pew, and make the house comfortable. Praise what is commendable, and let us all, in the spirit of Heb. 10: 24, 25, cultivate a more fervent type of piety.

7. How can we avoid the "long pauses" that drag and spoil a meeting? By each one having something to say or read, which he cannot permit the meeting to close without hearing. We ought to be willing to speak for Christ, even if we cannot imitate the accent of Cicero or the eloquence of Demosthenes. If we will only tell what we feel, we shall all be eloquent enough, and glorify God in the way pleasing to Him.

8. If our hearts are only full, we shall hardly be able to wait for our turn. Go to an exchange where

stocks are sold, and listen to the brokers all bidding at once, and learn the secret.

9. In moments of deep solemnity, it is very proper to give a moment or two to silent prayer. At the revival meetings conducted by our dear brethren, Major Whittle and Mr. Bliss, in our city in the Fall of 1876, I was much impressed with this custom, which they repeatedly used, and I am convinced that it did much good. During those moments of silent prayer, the house was so still that you could have heard a pin drop; yes, you could almost have heard your heart beat.

10. Let us enter into the spirit of the meeting. Sing " with grace in your heart to the Lord." Each prayer becomes our own if we follow it understandingly, and add to it a silent or audible " amen."

11. Do not wander from the topic, and begin a rehash of what you have said before a dozen times or so. A new topic each week admits of new thought, illustration and experience.

12. Have you no written requests for special prayer to bring to the prayer-meeting? If you have, hand these to the pastor, before the meeting. "If you have a special object of desire, ask others to join with you in seeking it. 'If two of you shall agree.'

Ask for something; give thanks for something; have a point in your prayer."

13. And when you receive the answer to your prayer, do not fail to speak of it, for this encourages others to pray, and confirms their faith.

14. Is it proper to cultivate the spirit of friendliness? If you are early and notice strangers, seek an introduction, or introduce yourself, and speak to them in words of welcome. Cannot you spend a few minutes after the close of the meeting for hand-shaking and the exchange of greetings with your friends and neighbors? Shake hands with as many as possible, and in every proper way cultivate the spirit of sociability. Why are you in such a hurry to go home from the prayer-meeting? Why cannot you spend several minutes in conversation about the topic, and in suggesting plans for work and greater usefulness! Would not such friendliness as this make the meetings social and delightful, and create the feeling that "it is good for us to be here?" It will be easy for you to speak a friendly word for Jesus now while the warmth of the meeting is upon you.

15. Let the opening remarks strike the key-note to the meeting. "Anybody can speak or pray when a meeting has become lively, interesting and

warm. Blessed is the man who dares to take hold of the cold end of a prayer-meeting."

16. Would it not, in case no other method has been adopted, add to the interest and profit, if the members during the continuation of the year would each select a dozen topics with three or more proof texts from Scripture such as are related to the wants, trials, and experiences of daily life—and then hand them to the pastor towards the end of the year? From these "themes from the pew," he would be able to pick out the right kind of topics for the wants of his people during the coming year : and certainly the people themselves would be bound to take an interest in topics of their own choosing.

CHAPTER XXIII.

Daily Prayer-Meeting Topics for 1878.

A very efficient aid for the improvement of the prayer-meeting, will be the selection of suitable topics. Accordingly we have introduced a number of lists which may serve as guides and hints in the selection at the outset. The entire number, with the list that follows, will include 572 subjects, or enough to supply a prayer-meeting for 11 years; and these subjects are as good for one year as for another. Or, if they are not used in this way, the study of these with their proof texts from the Scripture, will guide an individual church in the preparation of such topics as their special wants may demand. This list was prepared for the year 1878, by the Executive Committee of the Young Men's Christian Associations of the United States and the British Provinces.

TOPICS.

JANUARY.

1. Christ the Foundation. 1 Cor. 3: 9–16.
2. The Three Musts. John 3: 7, 14; Acts 4: 12.
3. The First Commandment. Ex. 20: 3; Isa. 43: 10–15.
4. The Stilling of the Tempest. Mark 4: 35–41.

5. Sunday-School Lesson. Rehoboam, First King of Judah: 2 Chron 12: 1–12; Golden Text: When he humbled himself, the wrath of the Lord turned from him. Verse 12.
7. Prayer. Prayer and Praise. Remembrance of personal and relative mercies; prayer for the divine blessing on past privileges, and for a humble and contrite spirit. Phil. 4: 6, 7; 1 Thess. 5: 17, 18.
8. Prayer. For the Church of Christ in all Lands: for its deliverance from error; for its increase in faith and holiness, and in power as a witness for the Lord Jesus Christ; for the grace and guidance of the Holy Spirit. Ps. 122.
9. Prayer. For Christian Families: for sick and afflicted members; for children at school, and for all youth in our colleges and seminaries of learning; for young men entering upon the active business of life, and for those abroad; for sons and daughters openly confessing Christ. Ps. 128.
10. Prayer. For Nations: for rulers, magistrates and statesmen; for the army and navy; for all benevolent and philanthropic institutions; for religious liberty and the opening of doors "wide and effectual" for publishing the Gospel; and for the reign of righteousness and peace. 1 Tim. 2; Isa. 1–8 35: 1, 2.
11. Prayer. For Christian Missions to the Jews and Gentiles: for Sunday-schools, and for the divine blessing on all Christian efforts to spread the glad tidings of the Gospel of Salvation. Matt. 28: 18–20; Isa. 52: 7–10.
12. Prayer. For the Circulation of the Bible: for the observance of the Sabbath; for the removal of intemperance; for the rescue of the fallen; for the safety of those who travel by land and by water. Acts 7: 38; Eze. .0: 12–20; Luke 4: 18, 19.
   Sunday-School Lesson. Asa Faithful to his God. 2 Chron. 14: 1–11; Golden Text: Lord it is nothing with thee to help, whether with many, or with them that have no power. Verse 11.
14. Working and Watching. Neh. 4: 1–11.
15. The Way of Life or of Death—Which? Josh. 24: 13 1 Kings 18: 21.
16. Is the Young Man Safe? 2 Sam. 18: 29–33.
17. The Sower. Luke 8: 5–8, 11–15.
18. God's Delight in Saving Sinners. Eze. 33: 11; Eph. 2: 4–8.
19. Sunday-School Lesson. The Covenant Renewed. 2 Chron. 8-15; Golden Text: Be ye strong, therefore, and let not your hands be weak: for your work shall be rewarded. Verse 7.

21. "Our Father, which art in heaven." Acts 17 : 22–31 ; Gal. 4 : 4–7.
22. The Gain of the Hypocrite. Job 27 : 8–10 ; Matt. 23 : 13.
23. "Seekest thou great things for thyself? Seek them not." Matt. 20 : 20–28 ; Mark 9 : 33–37.
24. Day of Prayer for Young Men in Colleges. Prov. 3 : 1–7.
25. "Come out of the man thou unclean spirit." Mark 5 : 1–20 ;
26. Sunday-School Lesson. Jehoshaphat's Prosperity. 2 Chron. 17 : 1–10 ; Golden Text : And they taught in Judah, and had the book of the law of the Lord with them, and went about throughout all the cities of Judah, and taught the people. Verse 9.
28. The Inspiration of the Bible. 2 Tim. 3 : 14–17 ; 2 Pet. 1 : 20, 21 ; 2 Sam. 23 : 1–3.
29. Whither art thou going—to Nineveh or Tarshish? Jonah 1.
30. Two Fearless Young Men. Num. 14 : 2–10 ; 32 : 10–12.
31. The Tenderness of God. Deut. 32 : 10–14.

FEBRUARY.

1. Promise Meeting. 2 Cor. 1 : 20. To the Sinner—John 6 : 37. To the Backslider—Jer. 3 : 22. To the Believer—Isa. 42 : 10, 13 ; Rev. 21 : 4.
2. Sunday-School Lesson. Jehoshaphat Reproved. 2 Chron. 19 : 1–9 ; Golden Text : There is no iniquity with the Lord our God, nor respect of persons, nor taking of gifts. Verse 7.
4. Self-Examination. 2 Cor. 13 : 5 ; Psa. 77 : 6 ; 2 Cor. 1–12.
5. "What wilt thou say when He shall punish thee?" Prov. 11 : 21 ; Nahum 1 : 2–8 ; 2 Cor. 5 : 10, 11 ; Lam. 3 : 39 ; Matt. 22 : 11, 12 ; Eccl. 8 : 11.
6. The Lord Looketh on the Heart. 1 Sam. 16 : 6, 7.
7. The Second Commandment. Ex. 20 : 4–6 ; Col. 3 : 1–5.
8. The Dead Brought to Life. Mark 5 : 22–24, 35–43.
9. Sunday-School Lesson. Jehoshaphat Helped of God. 2 Chron. 20 : 14–22 ; Golden Text : Believe in the Lord your God, so shall ye be established ; believe his prophets, so shall ye prosper. Verse 20.
11. "What think ye of Christ?" Matt. 22 : 42 ; Isa. 53 : 2 ; John 6 : 42 ; 3 : 2 ; Mark 8 : 29 ; John 20 : 28 ; 1 Pet. 2 : 7 ; Psa. 73 : 25.
12. Opportunities Neglected. Acts 24 : 24–27 ; 26 : 28.
13. A Promising Young Man, and how he Failed. 1 Sam. 9 : 2 ; 10 : 6, 7 ; 28 : 16–19.
14. Salvation in Christ alone. Acts 4 : 12 ; Isa. 45 : 10.

THE PRAYER-MEETING.

15. The Unending Misery of the Lost, and the Everlasting Joy of the Redeemed. Mark 9: 42-48; Isa. 35: 10.
16. Sunday-School Lesson. Joash Repairing the Temple. 2 Chron. 24: 4-13; Golden Text: Joash was minded to repair the house of the Lord. Verse 4.
18. "Hallowed be Thy name." Psa. 113: 1-3; Mal. 1: 11.
19. Salvation as a Gift. Rom. 6: 23; 1 John 5: 11.
20. Love Not the World. Eccl. 2: 1-11.
21. Sins of Thought Offensive to God. Gen. 6: 5-7; 1 John 3: 15.
22. Integrity in Civil Magistrates insisted on. Ex. 18: 21; Neh. 5: 15.
23. Sunday-School Lesson. Uzziah's Pride Punished. 2 Chron. 26: 16-23; Golden Text; Pride goeth before destruction, and a haughty spirit before a fall. Prov. 16: 18.
25. The Bible in the Public Meeting. Deut. 31: 10-13; Neh. 8: 1-8.
26. "After this the judgment." Acts 17: 32; Heb. 9: 27; Luke 12: 5.
27. A Young Man who made the right choice. Heb. 11: 24-27; Deut. 34: 10-12.
28. "While they are yet speaking, I will hear." Dan. 9: 21-23; Acts 12: 5-10; 4: 31; Luke 23: 42, 43.

MARCH.

1. The Cleansing of the Leper. Mark 1: 40-45.
2. Sunday-School Lesson. Ahaz' Persistent Wickedness. 2 Chron. 28: 19-27; Golden Text: And in the time of his distress did he trespass yet more against the Lord: this is that King Ahaz. Verse 22.
4. Sound Doctrine Enjoined. 2 Tim. 4: 1-4; 1 Tim. 4: 16; John 7: 17.
5. Christ the Way. John 14: 6; Heb. 10: 19-23.
6. Ash Wednesday. "Rend your heart, and not your garments." Joel 2: 12-19, Psa. 51: 17.
7. The Third Commandment. Ex. 29: 7; Matt. 5: 33-37.
8. Christ's Tenderness to the Fallen. Luke 7: 36-50.
9. Sunday-School Lesson. Hezekiah's Good Reign. 2 Chron. 29: 1-11; Golden Text: And in every work that he began . . . he did it with all his heart and prospered. 2 Chron. 31: 21.
11. Brotherly Love. 1 John 4: 11-21.
12. I am Guilty and Need Pardon. Rom. 3: 23-26.
13. Blessedness of the Man who Delights in the Word. Psa. 1: 1-3; James 1: 25.

14. The Draw-net. Matt. 13: 47–50.
15. The Healing of the Centurion's Servant. Luke 7: 1–10.
16. Sunday-School Lesson. Hezekiah and the Assyrians. 2 Chron. 32: 9–21; Golden Text: With him is an arm of flesh; but with us is the Lord our God, to help us, and to fight our battles. Verse 8.
18. "Thy kingdom come." Psa. 2; Rev. 11: 15–17.
19. Christ the Truth. 1 John 5: 20; John 17: 3.
20. The Good Fight. 1 Tim. 6: 12; 2 Tim. 4: 7, 8.
21. Confession called out. Mark 5: 25–34.
22. State of the Unsaved. Dead—Eph. 2: 1. Lost—Luke 19: 10. Condemned—John 3: 19. Children of Wrath—Eph. 2: 3. Without God—Eph. 2: 12.
23. Sunday-School Lesson. Manasseh Brought to Repentance. 2 Chron. 33: 9–16; Golden Text: As many as I love, I rebuke and chasten: be zealous, therefore, and repent. Rev. 3: 19.
25. Christ our Substitute. John 1: 29; Heb. 9: 28; Gal. 2: 20; 2 Cor. 5: 21.
26. National Disobedience. 1 Sam. 12: 15; Jer. 12: 17.
27. Tampering with Sin. Judges 16: 4–20.
28. Duties of Employers. Col. 4: 1; Eph. 6: 9.
29. The Man with the Unclean Spirit. Mark 1: 23–27.
30. Sunday-School Lesson. Review of the Lessons for the Quarter.

APRIL.

1. Forbearing grace. Luke 13: 6–9.
2. Christ the Life. John 6: 33–40.
3. "None Righteous." Rom. 3: 10–18; Eccl. 7: 20.
4. The Fourth Commandment. Ex. 20: 8–11; Jer. 17: 19–27.
5. Is God Ready to Pardon Me Now? Psa. 86: 5; Isa. 1: 18–20; 2 Cor. 6: 2.
6. Sunday-School Lesson. Josiah's Early Piety. 2 Chron. 34: 1–8; Golden Text: Remember now thy Creator in the days of thy youth, while the evil days come not, nor the years draw nigh, when thou shalt say, I have no pleasure in them. Eccl. 12: 1.
8. Power of the Prayer of Faith. Josh. 10: 12, 13; James 5: 16–18; 1 John 5: 14, 15.
9. The New Heart. Eze. 36: 26; Acts 15: 9.
10. A Young Man who Found Favor with God and Man. Gen. 41: 12, 13, 38–45.
11. Duties of the Employed. Col. 3: 22–25; Titus 2: 9, 10.

THE PRAYER-MEETING. 201

12. "Wilt thou be made whole?" John 5 : 1-16.
13. Sunday-School Lesson. The Scriptures Found and Searched. 2 Chron. 34 : 14-22 ; Golden Text, John 5 : 39.
15. "Thy will be done." Matt. 7 : 21 ; Rom. 2 : 13.
16. What to Lay Off, and What to Put On. Col. 3 : 8-15.
17. How can a Man be Born Again? By Believing—1 John 5 : 1. By Receiving—John 1 : 12, 13. By the Spirit—Titus 3 : 5. By the Word of God—James 1 : 18.
18. "Cast the net on the right side." John 21 : 1-13.
19. Good Friday. Isa. 52 : 13-15 ; 53 : 1-12.
20. Sunday-School Lesson. Jeremiah in Prison. Jer. 33 : 1-9 ; Golden Text, verse 3.
22. Easter Monday. Matt. 28 : 1-20.
23. The Sinner's Wealth Rom. 2 : 5-9.
24. One who Trusted in Something Better than his Own Good Works. Phil. 3 : 4-11.
25. The Unmerciful Servant. Matt. 18 : 21-35.
26. "Lord, save me." Matt. 14 : 22-33.
27. Sunday-School Lesson. The Rechabites. Jer. 35 : 12-19 ; Golden Text, verse 13.
+ 29. "God is our refuge." Psa. 46.
30. The Wicked Husbandmen. Mark 12 : 1-12.

MAY.

1. A Personal Saviour. Phil. 3. 10; 2 Tim. 1 : 12.
2. The Believer's Home. Rev. 21 : 25 ; 3 : 12 ; Psa. 17 : 15.
3. The Compassion of Jesus. Matt. 9 : 35-38.
4. Sunday-School Lesson. The Captivity of Judah. Jer. 52 : 1-11 ; Golden Text, Lam. 1 : 8.
+ 6. "Now." Luke 14 : 17 ; 2 Cor. 6 : 2 ; Rom. 8 : 1 ; 1 John 3 : 2.
7. I am a Rebel, and need to be Restored to the Divine Favor. Rom. 3 : 10-12 ; Isa. 53 : 6.
8. A Young Man who Despised the Promises of God. Gen. 25 : 27-34 ; Heb. 12 : 16, 17.
9. Laborers in the Vineyard. Matt. 20 : 1-16.
10. The Woman Loosed from her Infirmity. Luke 13 : 10-17 ; Psa. 145 : 14.
11. Sunday-School Lesson. The Captives in Babylon. Dan. 1 : 8-17 ; Golden Text, Psa. 111 : 10.
13. The Testimony of the Man Born Blind. John 9.
14. Choose. Deut. 30 : 15-19.
15. We Must Forsake our Sins. Isa. 55 : 7 ; Eze. 18 : 30-32.
16. The Ten Virgins. Matt. 25 : 1-13.
17. Able to Keep. Psa. 121 ; Jude 24.
18. Sunday-School Lesson. Nebuchadnezzar's Dream. Dan. 2 : 36-45 ; Golden Text, verse 28.

20. Searching the Scriptures. John 5 : 38-40 ; Acts 17 : 11, 12.
21. God as a Suppliant. Hosea 11 : 1-9 ; Isa. 65 : 2.
22. Christ an Example of Humility. John 13 : 1-15.
23. Unbelief. Psa. 78 : 17-22 ; 1 John 5 : 10, 11
24. The Withered Hand Restored. Luke 6 : 6-11.
25. Sunday-School Lesson. The Fiery Furnace. Dan. 3 : 21-27. Golden Text, verse 17.
27. Christ Coming for His Saints. John 14 : 1-3 ; 1 Cor. 15 : 51-54 ; 1 Thess. 4 : 13-18.
28. "But they made light of it." Luke 14 : 15-24.
29. The Prizes of Christian Warfare. Rev. 3 : 5, 12, 21.
30. Ascension Day. Luke 24 : 46-53.
31. Encouraging Promises. Matt. 9 : 29 ; Rom. 10 : 9 ; Matt. 10 : 22 ; James 1 : 12.

JUNE.

1. Sunday-School Lesson. The Handwriting on the Wall. Dan. 5 : 22-31 ; Golden Text : Thou art weighed in the balances, and art found wanting. Verse 27.
3. Self-Denial. Gen. 12 : 1-5 ; Heb. 11 : 8-10.
4. How shall the Sinner Escape ? Heb. 2 : 3 ; 1 Pet. 4 : 18.
5. Evil Thoughts—How can I be delivered from them ? Matt. 15 : 19, 20 ; 2 Cor. 10 : 5.
6. The Fifth Commandment. Ex. 20 : 12 ; Luke 2 : 51.
7. Self-purification Impossible. Jer. 2 : 22 ; 13 : 23 ; Prov. 20 : 9.
8. Sunday-School Lesson. Daniel in the Lions' Den. Dan. 6 : 14-23 ; Golden Text : My God hath sent his angel, and hath shut the lions' mouths, that they have not hurt me. Verse 22.
10. What Christ Does for the Believer. He Dies for Me—John 10 : 11. He Seeks Me—Eze. 34 : 11. He Gives Me Rest —Psa. 23 : 2 (first clause). He Knows Me—John 10 : 27. He Leads Me—Psa. 23 : 2 (last clause). He Carries Me. Isa. 40 : 11. He Feeds Me—John 21 : 15. He Heals Me—Eze. 34 : 16. He Makes Me a Blessing—Eze. 34 : 26. He Comes for Me—John 14 : 3.
11. Seek ye the Lord. Amos 5 : 4-8.
12. The Temple of God. 2 Cor. 6 : 16 ; 1 Cor. 3 : 16, 17.
13. "Where are the nine ?" Luke 17 : 11-19.
14. The Sinner Invited. Matt. 11 : 28-30 ; John 6 : 37.
15. Sunday-School Lesson. Messiah's Kingkom. Dan. 7 : 9-14 ; Golden Text : Thy throne, O God, is for ever and ever ; the sceptre of thy kingdom is a right sceptre. Psa. 45 : 6.
17. The Word a Light. Psa. 119 : 105, 130 ; Prov. 6 : 23.
18. A Promise Given, and a Choice Required. Jer. 29 : 13 ; Matt. 6 : 24.

THE PRAYER-MEETING. 203

- 19. On What are You Building? Matt. 7 : 24-29.
- \+ 20. Fruitfulness. John 15 : 1-5.
- 21. "If thou canst believe." Mark 9 : 14-29.
- 22. Sunday-School Lesson. The Decree of Cyrus. 2 Chron. 36 : 22-23; Golden Text: Speak ye comfortably to Jerusalem, and cry unto her, that her warfare is accomplished, that her iniquity is pardoned. Isa. 40 : 2.
- 24. "Give us this day our daily bread." Prov. 30 : 8, 9 ; Ps. 34 : 10.
- 25. An Important Question Answered. Psa. 15.
- 26. My Besetting Sin—How can I get Strength to Overcome it? Heb. 12 : 1-4 ; 1 Cor. 9 : 27.
- 27. The Christian in the World. Matt. 5 : 13-16.
- 28. Decision Necessary to the Service of God. 2 Chron. 15 : 12; Luke 9 : 62.
- 29. Sunday-School Lesson. Review of the Lessons for the Quarter.

JULY.

- 1. The Work of the Spirit. 1 Cor. 2 : 9-16 ; Rom. 8 : 14-17.
- 2. Where is thy Brother? Gen. 4 : 9; Eze. 33 : 8-9.
- 3. What Christ says to Every Unconverted Young Man. Luke 7 : 11-16.
- 4. God's Children Free. John 8 : 31-36.
- 5. The Raising of Lazarus. John 11 : 1-45.
- 6. Sunday-School Lesson. Birth of Christ the Lord. Luke 2 : 8-20 ; Golden Text: For unto you is born this day, in the city of David, a Saviour, which is Christ the Lord. Verse 11.
- 8. Christ Coming with His Saints. 2 Thess. 1 : 7-10; Col. 3 : 4 ; Jude 14, 15.
- 9. "Wait on the Lord." Lam. 3 : 25, 26 ; Isa. 40 : 28-31.
- 10. Invitations Refused. Luke 14 : 15-24 ; Prov. 1 : 24-28.
- 11. "Give ye them to eat." Luke 9 : 12-17 ; John 21 : 15-17.
- 12. Christ's Willingness to Receive Sinners. Luke 15 : 2 ; John 6 : 37; Luke 9 : 11.
- 13. Sunday-School Lesson. The Childhood of Jesus. Luke 2 : 40-52 ; Golden Text, verse 52.
- 15. Christ is Able To: Perform all he Promises—Rom. 4: 21. Save to the Uttermost—Heb 7 : 25. Make Stand—Rom. 14 : 4. Keep from Falling—Jude 24. Keep what is Committed to Him—2 Tim. 1 : 12. Succor the Tempted. —Heb. 2 : 18. Make all Grace Abound—2 Cor. 9: 8. Do Exceeding Abundantly—Eph. 3 : 20.
- 16. "All that believe are justified." Acts 13 : 38, 39 ; Gal. 2 : 16; Rom. 4 : 5.
- 17. Seeking the Lost. Luke 19 : 1-10.
- 18. The Sixth Commandment. Ex. 20 : 13 ; Matt. 5 : 21, 22.

19. "Have mercy on me." Mark 10:46-52.
20. Sunday-School Lesson. Ministry of John the Baptist. Luke 3:15-22; Golden Text, Luke 1:15.
22. The Word Made Plain. Psa. 119:18; Eph. 1:17-23.
23. Good News—Poor Men Made Rich. Isa. 55:1-3; Rev. 21:7.
24. In What Men should Glory. Jer. 9:23, 24; Gal. 6:14.
25. The Law of Growth in the Kingdom of God. Mark 4:26-29; 2 Pet. 3:18.
26. Invitation to All. Rev. 22:17; 2 Cor. 5:20, 21; 6:1, 2.
27. Sunday-School Lesson. Jesus at Nazareth. Luke 4:16-30; Golden Text, verse 32.
29. The Lord our Helper. Psa. 20; Deut. 31:6-8.
30. "Learn of me." Matt. 11:29.
31. Evil Effects of Bad Company. Gen. 13:12, 13; 19:1, 12-28.

AUGUST.

1. "Humbleness of mind." Col. 3:12-14.
2. The Healing of One Deaf and Dumb. Mark 7:31-37.
3. Sunday-School Lesson. The Draught of Fishes. Luke 5:1-11 Golden Text, verse 11.
5. The Weapon of Our Warfare. Eph. 6:17. Heb. 4:12; Jer. 23:29.
6. The Rich Fool. Luke 12:16-21.
7. An Ambitious Young Man and his Untimely End. 2 Sam. 15:1-5, 13, 14; 18:6-15.
8. The Seventh Commandment. Ex. 20:14; Eph. 5:3-7.
9. Victory over the Devil. Gen. 3:15; Matt. 4:1-11; 1 John 2:14.
10. Sunday-School Lesson. The Centurion's Faith. Luke 7:1-10; Golden Text: According to your faith be it unto you. Matt. 9:29.
12. Despising the Word. Heb. 2:1-3; Prov. 13:13.
13. Two Companies and Two Ends. Matt. 7:13, 14; Ex. 23:2; Heb. 12:22-24; Luke 16:22, 23.
14. What it is to know Christ. John 17:3; Phil. 3:7-11.
15. Hearing God's Call. 1 Sam. 3:1-10.
16. "He will abundantly pardon." Isa. 55:7; Neh. 9:16, 17.
17. Sunday-School Lesson. The Widow of Nain. Luke 7:11-17; Golden Text: And when the Lord saw her, He had compassion on her, and said unto her, weep not. Verse 13.
19. Christ Coming in Judgment. Matt. 25:31-46.
20. "Escape for thy life." Gen. 19:15-17.
21. Young Men—their Rule for Right Living. Psa. 119:9; Josh. 1:8.
22. Duties of Parents to Children. Eph. 6:4; Deut. 6:6-9.

THE PRAYER-MEETING.   205

23. The Great Change. Zech. 3 : 1–7.
24. Sunday-School Lesson. The Friend of Sinners. Luke 7 : 40-50; Golden Text : Luke 15 : 2.
26. Seven Results of Abiding in Christ. Fruit, Answered Prayer, Love, Obedience, Joy, Fellowship, Service. John 15 : 5–16.
27. The Lost Piece of Money. Luke 15 : 1, 2, 8–10.
28. Individual Responsibility. 2 Cor. 5 : 10; Rom. 14 : 10–12.
29. The Waiting Lord. Rev. 3 : 20 ; Song of Sol., 5 : 2.
30. Christ Lives in the Believer. Gal. 2 : 20 ; Eph. 3 : 14–21.
31. Sunday-School Lesson. Return of the Seventy. Luke 10 : 17–24 ; Golden Text, verse 23.

September.

2. "He opened to us the Scriptures." Luke 24 : 13–32.
3. The Way Out of the Ditch. Jer. 3 : 12 13; Hosea 14 : 1–4.
4. "Your Sins will Find You Out." Num. 32 : 23 ; Gen. 44 : 16–34.
5. The Eighth Commandment. Ex. 20 : 15; Lev. 19 : 11–13.
6. Christ's Help in Temptation. Heb. 2 : 18; 2 Cor. 12 : 9.
7. Sunday-School Lesson. The Good Samaritan. Luke 10 : 30–37. Golden Text : Gal. 5 : 14.
9. "Forgive us our debts as we forgive our debtors." Mark 11 : 25 ; 18 : 21, 22.
10. Idleness. Prov. 24 : 30–34.
11. An Exhortation to a Young Man. 1 Tim. 4 : 12–16.
12. Love the Impulse to Labor. John 21 : 15–17 ; 2 Cor. 5 : 14, 15.
13. Invitation to the Thirsty. Isa. 55 : 1–9.
14. Sunday-School Lesson Importunity in Prayer. Luke 11 : 5–13 ; Golden Text : Luke 18 : 1.
16. God the Deliverer of His People. Ex. 14 : 10–31.
17. The Sinner's Condemnation. John 3 : 17–21.
18. A Zeal for Christ which consumes Self. Luke 9 : 23 ; 2 Cor. 5 : 14, 15 ; 1 Thess. 2 : 8.
19. The Aged—Prayer and Promise. Prov. 16 : 31 ; Psa. 71 : 1–19 ; Isa. 46 : 4.
20. "Do all to the glory of God." 1 Cor. 10 : 31–33 ; Rom. 15 : 3.
21. Sunday-School Lesson. Warning against Covetousness. Luke 12 : 13–23 ; Golden Text, verse 15.
23. Indwelling and Comfort of the Holy Spirit. John 20 : 22 ; Acts 2 : 4 ; John 16 : 7–13.
24. Christ's Mission. 1 Tim. 1 : 15.
25. True to God, regardless of Consequences. Dan. 3 : 13–30.
26. Neglect of the Poor a Neglect of Christ. Matt. 25 : 42–45 ; Mark 9 : 41.

27. Nothing too Hard for God. Jer. 32 : 17 ; Psa. 130 : 1–5.
28. Sunday-School Lesson. Review of the Lessons for the Quarter.
30. God's Word in Us. Col. 3 : 16 ; Psa. 119 : 11 ; Jer. 20 : 9.

OCTOBER.

1. Too Late. Luke 19 : 41–44 ; Heb. 3 : 17-19.
2. Wisdom. Prov. 2 : 1-9 ; James 1 : 5.
3. The Ninth Commandment. Ex. 20 : 16 ; Psa. 15 : 1-4.
4. Sowing and Reaping. Gal. 6 : 7, 8.
5. Sunday-School Lesson. Warning against Formalism. Luke 13 : 22-30 ; Golden Text, verse 24.
7. Tokens of Our Love to God. John 14 : 21-23 ; 1 John 2 : 15.
8. Jabez' Prayer. 1 Chron. 4 : 9, 10.
9. A Young Man who Sought only this World's Joys. Luke 15 : 11-24.
10. The Question Every Man must Answer. Matt. 27 : 22.
11. The Saviour we need Offered. Rom. 3 : 10-26.
12. Sunday-School Lesson. The Gospel Feast. Luke 14 : 15-24 ; Golden Text, verse 15.
14. Things we Know. Rom. 7 : 18 ; 2 Tim. 1 : 12 ; 1 John 5 : 13 ; Rom. 8 : 28.
15. Safe Voyage, if Christ is on Board. Mark 4 : 35-41.
16. Whole-hearted for Christ. Luke 9 : 57-62.
17. "At Thy word I will let down the net." Luke 5 : 1-11.
18. Exhortation to Watchfulness. 1 Thess. 5 : 6-8.
19. Sunday-School Lesson. The Prodigal Son. Luke 15 : 11-24 ; Golden Text : Psa. 40 : 17.
21. "Lead us not into temptation, but deliver us from evil." Jas. 1 : 13-15 ; 1 Cor. 10 : 13 ; 2 Pet. 2 : 9 ; 2 Tim. 4 : 18.
22. The Two Future States. Luke 16 : 19-31.
23. How a Young Man made his Life Successful. Acts 7 : 57-59 ; 26 : 9-23 ; 2 Cor. 5 : 13, 14.
24. The Pharisee and the Publican. Luke 18 : 9-14.
25. "The Lamb of God." John 1 : 29 ; Rev. 5 : 12, 13 ; 6 : 15-17.
26. Sunday-School Lesson. The Rich Man and Lazarus. Luke 16 : 19-31 ; Golden Text : Prov. 14 : 32.
28. Teaching and Keeping God's Word. Deut. 11 : 18-25.
29. The Call to the Backslider. Jer. 2 : 5, 13, 19 ; 3 : 12-14.
30. Ruined by Evil Company. 2 Chron. 10 : 1-14 ; 12 : 14-16.
31. Profession without Fruit an Offence. Mark 11 : 12-14 ; John 15 : 2.

NOVEMBER.

1. The Wanderer's Cry. Psa. 51.
2. Sunday-School Lesson. The Ten Lepers. Luke 17 : 11-19 ; Golden Text, verse 17.

THE PRAYER-MEETING. 207

4. Promise Meeting. 2 Pet. 1:4; Matt. 28:20; Acts 1:8; John 14:3.
5. Who are Haters of God? John 15:17-25; Rom. 8:7, 8.
6. A Young Man's Wise Choice. 1 Kings 3:5-14.
7. The Tenth Commandment. Ex. 20:17; Heb. 13:5.
8. "We will hear thee again." Acts 17:32; Prov. 27:1.
9. Sunday-School Lesson. Whom the Lord Receives. Luke 18:9-17; Golden Text, verse 17.
11. Young Men — their Power for Evil. 1 Kings 11:28; 12:26-30; 13:33, 34; Acts 7:57-59; 8:1-3.
12. Young Men—their Power for Good. Prov. 20:29; 1 John 2:13, 14; Eph. 6:10, 11.
13. Something Stronger than the Strength of Young Men. Isa. 40:28-31.
14. How to Reach Young Men. John 1:35-46.
15. Young Men — their Special Temptations. Eccl. 11:9, 10; 2 Tim. 2:22.
16. The Pattern for Young Men. Luke 2:42-52; Acts 10:38-43, Sunday-School Lesson. Zaccheus, the Publican. Luke 19:1-10; Golden Text, verse 10.
18. Baptism of the Spirit for Service. Acts 1:8; 2:4; 4:31.
19. When do men cry unto the Lord? Psa. 107:5, 6, 12, 13, 18, 19, 27, 28.
20. A Life Well Begun. 2 Chron. 34:1-8, 29-33.
21. The Lesson of Patience. James 5:7-11.
22. Invitation and Warning. Isa. 1:18; Prov. 1:24-33.
23. Sunday-School Lesson. Judaism Overthrown. Luke 21:8-21; Golden Text: Luke 19:41.
25. Profit in Using the Word. 2 Tim. 3:12-16; Isa. 55:10, 11.
26. Repentance. Matt. 9:13; Eze. 18:32; Acts 5:31.
27. A Young Man in whom the World found no fault, except his Religion. Dan. 6:1-5, 25-28; Phil. 2:15.
28. "The Sacrifice of Praise." Psa. 148; Rev. 7:11; Heb. 13:15, 16.
29. Halting Between Two Opinions. 1 Kings 18:21; Joshua 24:15.
30. Sunday-School Lessons. The Lord's Supper. Luke 22:10-20; Golden Text: 1 Cor. 11:26.

DECEMBER.

2. The Imagination. Corrupt—Rom. 1:21; Deut. 29:19, 20. Redeemed—Isa. 26:3; ("Mind," in margin "imagination" or "thought"). Phil. 4:7.
3. God our our Searcher. Psa. 139:23, 24; 1 Chron. 28:9.

4. Some Things Money Cannot Buy. Redemption—1 Pet. 1: 18, 19. The Gift of the Spirit—Acts 8: 18-23. The Heavenly Inheritance—1 Pet. 3-5.
5. The Pounds. Luke 19: 11-27.
6. I am a Slave to Sin and need to be Set Free. Heb. 2: 14, 15; Phil. 2: 7-9.
7. Sunday-School Lesson. The Cross. Luke 23: 33-46; Golden Text: Gal. 6: 14.
9. Justification. Isa. 53: 11; Rom. 8: 33; Rom. 5: 8, 9.
10. Grieve not the Holy Spirit. Gen. 6: 3; 1 Thess. 5: 19; Isa. 63: 10.
11. A Young Man's Foolish Choice. Mark 10: 17: 22.
12. Idle Words. Matt. 12: 36; Eph. 4: 29-31.
13. Joy over Deliverance. Acts 8: 5-8.
14. Sunday-School Lesson. The Walk to Emmaus. Luke 24: 13-32; Golden Text, verse 32.
16. The Word "written that ye may believe." John 20: 31; 2 Tim. 3: 15.
17. A Sinner Awakened and Saved. Acts 16: 22-34.
18. Christ as a Pattern for Young Men. Phil. 2: 5-16.
19. Riches do not Satisfy. Eccl 5: 10, 11; Psa. 49: 11-13; 1 Tim. 6: 17-19.
20. Help Cometh from God. Psa. 89: 19; 142: 4, 5.
21. Sunday-School Lesson. The Saviour's Last Words. Luke 24: 44-53; Golden Text: Matt. 28: 20.
23. Christ the Fulfilment of Scripture. Matt. 5: 17; Luke 24: 27; Rev. 19: 10.
24. Redemption. Gal. 4: 4, 5; 1 Pet. 1: 18, 19.
25. Glad Tidings. Luke 2: 1-20.
26. "Think on these Things." Phil. 4: 8, 9; Heb. 2: 1.
27. "Mighty to Save." Isa 63: 1.
28. Sunday-School Lesson. Review of the Lessons for the Quarter.
30. "For Thine is the kingdom, the power and the glory." 1 Chron. 29: 10-13; Psa. 62: 11; Rev. 5: 13.
31. How shall we Number Our Days and Years? Psa. 90: 12; Eccl. 9: 10; Eph. 5: 15-17.

"Did not our heart burn within us, while He talked with us by the way, and while He opened to us the Scriptures?" (Luke 24: 32.)

"Now unto him that is able to keep you from falling, and to present you faultless before the presence of his glory with exceeding joy, to the only wise God our Saviour, be glory and majesty, dominion and power, both now and forever. Amen."

W. G. HOLMES,

Publisher and Bookseller,

77 MADISON STREET, CHICAGO,

Has a very large assortment of Books designed as helps in the study of the Scriptures; including BIBLICAL ENCYCLOPEDIAS, AND DICTIONARIES; COMMENTARIES on the whole and various parts of Scripture; HAND-BOOKS OF STUDY; MAPS of the Holy Land; TOPICAL STUDIES; BIBLE CLASS MANUALS; and many Helps and Guides for Sunday-school Teachers and Bible Students. Also, a VERY COMPLETE VARIETY OF THE BAGSTER AND TEACHERS' BIBLES.

www.ingramcontent.com/pod-product-compliance
Lightning Source LLC
Chambersburg PA
CBHW020859230426
43666CB00008B/1241